Kiwi Heroes

50 Courageous New Zealanders

Kiwi Heroes

50 Courageous New Zealanders

Bronwyn Sell

A&U

To Solomon from Uncle Terry Xmas '10

First published in 2010

Allen & Unwin
83 Alexander Street
Crows Nest NSW 2065
Australia
Phone: (61 2) 8425 0100
Fax: (61 2) 9906 2218
Email: info@allenandunwin.com
Web: www.allenandunwin.com

National Library of New Zealand Cataloguing-in-Publication Data
Sell, Bronwyn, 1974-
Kiwi heroes : 50 courageous New Zealanders / Bronwyn Sell.
Includes bibliographical references.
ISBN 978-1-877505-03-4
1. Heroes—New Zealand. 2. Courage—New Zealand.
I. Title.
920.093—dc 22

Set in 11.5 Rotis Serif
Designed and typeset by Janet Hunt
Cover designed by Nick Turzynski, redinc

Cover image courtesy of the Alexander Turnbull Library, Wellington

Printed in Australia by Griffin Press

10 9 8 7 6 5 4 3 2 1

FSC © Mixed Sources
Product group from well-managed forests, and other controlled sources
www.fsc.org Cert no. SGS-COC-005088
© 1996 Forest Stewardship Council

The paper in this book is FSC certified. FSC promotes environmentally responsible, socially beneficial and economically viable management of the world's forests.

Contents

3. CRUSADERS

4. IDEALISTS

Introduction: the mark of a hero

Ask any New Zealander to name the greatest Kiwi hero in history and there's a good chance the reply will be, 'Sir Edmund Hillary'.

But imagine for a moment if Hillary had been an arrogant, greedy man; if he had descended from his historic Mt Everest climb in 1953 boasting of his courage and skill; if he had used his public profile to line his own pockets; if he had been rude to schoolchildren and impatient with admirers; if he had insisted people call him 'Sir Edmund' rather than simply, 'Ed'.

Would we still consider him a hero?

Granted, Hillary climbed a very high mountain. And, yes, that was a great accomplishment. But only afterwards–long afterwards–did he truly become a hero.

Hillary was a hero not because he was the first man to stand on the world's tallest peak. He was a hero because he devoted the rest of his life to improving the lives of the Nepalese people–at great financial and personal cost. He was a hero because he never considered himself to be any better than anyone else; he calmly absorbed the international fame that came with his Everest status but he was as legendary for his humility as for his mountaineering ability.

'You don't have to be a fantastic hero to do certain things,' he once said. 'You can be just an ordinary chap, sufficiently motivated to reach challenging goals. The intense effort, the giving of everything you've got, is a very pleasant bonus.'

He was talking about the act of competing but it also nicely sums up that other remarkable aspect of his life: philanthropy. Hillary considered his greatest accomplishment to be not the Everest climb, but the work he did later on behalf of the Sherpas of Nepal.

The *New Zealand Oxford Dictionary* defines 'hero' as: 'a person noted or admired for nobility, courage, outstanding achievements, etc. (*Newton, a hero of science*).'

Our definition, for the purposes of this book, is a little narrower. We added an element of sacrifice. All our heroes were prepared to take great risks—to put themselves in the firing line, literally or metaphorically—for the benefit of others. By this definition an iconic figure is not necessarily a hero. Had he been a New Zealander, Newton probably wouldn't have made our shortlist.

Motivation was also a key factor. Our heroes knew the risks but chose to take them anyway. We had a philosophical discussion about whether a dog could demonstrate motivation. (We decided it could, thus you'll find a remarkable story within these pages about a terrier called George.)

Our final cut is by no means an exhaustive or definitive list. It would take a book of Britannia proportions to cover every hero in New Zealand history.

Many of these people are household names but some are barely known outside their own households. Some have become heroes because of a decision made in the heat of a moment, some because of the efforts of a lifetime.

Some are soldiers and firefighters who've gone beyond the call of duty, some are ordinary people who've been plunged into terrifying circumstances and responded with astonishing bravery. Some, including Hillary, are people who've selflessly devoted their lives to their principles and endured formidable hardships for the greater good. Many have forfeited their lives, their reputations or their livelihoods for the sake of others.

Kiwi Heroes tells the stories of some of the bravest people this country has produced: from Royd Kennedy, the firefighter who crawled under a blazing tanker to comfort a trapped little girl; to Ettie Rout, who was publicly vilified for her campaign to protect our soldiers from venereal disease in World War I; to Nancy Wake, the socialite wife who joined the French resistance and ran an army of guerrilla fighters to sabotage Nazi efforts in World War II; to Tony McClean, the young teacher who became trapped in a flooded gorge and hooked a disabled student to him before jumping into the torrid water, knowing he was compromising his own chances of survival.

Jan Morris, the journalist on the 1953 expedition to Everest, once wrote of Hillary and his fellow climber Tenzing Norgay:

'I liked these men very much when I first met them on the mountain nearly a half-century ago, but I came to admire them far more in the years that followed. I thought their brand of heroism—the heroism of example, the heroism of debts repaid and causes sustained—far more inspiring than the gung-ho kind.'

It's fitting to leave the last word here to Hillary: 'People do not decide to become extraordinary. They decide to accomplish extraordinary things.'

1.

RESCUERS

Huria Matenga
Hemi Matenga
Hohapeta Kahupuku

The saviours of the Delaware

It was one of the worst storms Huria Matenga had seen in her 22 years. At daybreak on 4 September 1863 the sky barely lightened. Winds blasted her home at Wakapuaka, near Nelson, rain thrashed the air and waves thundered against towering cliffs in the bay below.

By 9 a.m. a ship lay groaning against the rocks in the bay, each mountainous wave pounding it closer to oblivion. Upon spotting it, Matenga, her husband Hemi and his relation, Hohapeta Kahupuku, sprinted down to the shoreline.

Aboard the *Delaware*, a newly built brigantine that had set sail from Nelson for Hawke's Bay the previous day, the crew were desperate. They had tried to round both the northern and southern headlands of the bay but had been pushed back by the violent onshore wind and the thumping sea. Having lost their jib in the night, they had tried to anchor, but the rolling waves had made it impossible for their main anchor to hold, and its chain had snapped. The captain, Robert Baldwin, had made the difficult decision to beach the drifting ship, to at least save the crew and perhaps the cargo, but they'd hit submerged rocks some 100 to 150 metres from shore. The ship's rowboats had been swiftly swept away and destroyed. The crew had clung on helplessly as their ship broke in two on the rocks.

Now, their only chance of survival was to get a line to shore—a good thick rope tied fast to the deck that could be anchored on to rocks on the beach. It would provide a guide line that the men on board could cling to as they heaved themselves ashore, one by one. (Accounts of the number on board vary, from 10 to 32.)

With no boats, there was no way to get the line out except to swim for it—through huge seas that were smashing up against rocks that loomed up everywhere. The mate, wiry 22-year-old Englishman Henry Squirrel, volunteered. Though he'd only days before been released from Nelson Hospital after a two-week illness, he was a strong swimmer.

His crewmates tied a line around his waist and he lowered himself into the swirling water. He'd barely got wet when a wave bashed the ship—and him—against the rocks.

'Oh the rock, oh the rock,' he cried. He fell into the water and started floating away. The captain threw him first one life buoy, then another, but he was too senseless to grab them.

Realising the line was still secured around Squirrel's legs, the captain ordered able seaman William Morgan to haul him back up. He was apparently lifeless, his body an unresponsive heap. The crew tried to resuscitate him but he didn't respond. Morgan, with help from his shipmates, laid him on a bunk in the forecastle, and swiftly returned to the deck.

It seemed like suicide for anyone else to attempt what the mate had tried. But, just as all seemed lost, they spotted the three hazy figures on the rough strip of beach. Their best chance was to throw the rope to them—but the distance was too great. And a boiling stretch of sea lay between them.

Hemi Matenga later recalled: 'We men [he and Kahupuku]

thought it was impossible to reach the ship; the beach there is very treacherous with a swirling backwash; it seemed madness to face that sea.'

His wife had other ideas. She stripped off her heavier clothing and plunged into the water. She fought through the breakers, inch by inch, until she reached a rock near the ship. She clambered up and Morgan threw her the line, just as her kinsmen caught up with her. Morgan and the three rescuers used the rope to haul a stronger cable into shore, where it was secured to a rock.

Morgan was the first off the ship, clinging by arms and legs to the rope as he pulled himself through the crashing surf. One moment he'd be tossed up into the air, the next, as the ship rolled, he'd be plunged into the foaming water. As he neared the shore, the local trio waded into the waves, which at times crashed above their heads, to help him on to the beach.

From the ship, Captain Baldwin watched as the rest of his crew and his sole passenger followed Morgan. When all were safe, Baldwin went to check on the injured Squirrel, ignoring shouts from the shore that the rope was fraying and the boat's keel was out of the water.

He lifted the mate's eyelids, but there was no doubt in his mind: the brave young man was dead.

As waves surged over the ship, the heavy-hearted captain followed his crew's route down the rope—and just in time. As he was nearing the shore it released its hold on the ship and he was left flailing in the surf. The Maori trio caught him and dragged him to safety.

Safe on the beach at last, the captain collapsed and, in Morgan's words, 'cried like a child' for his lost friend and his lost ship.

He and the crew sat on the stony shore and watched, stunned, as their vessel was torn apart. Huria, Hemi and Hohapeta, who'd by then been joined by two other locals, lit a fire and gave them dry clothes, blankets and food.

After about an hour several of the crew shouted out at once. The captain too saw what they had spotted—movement aboard the ship. Squirrel had dragged himself out of the bed and was clinging to the fore-rigging as the vessel, now lying on its side, rose and fell in the swell. He cried out for help.

With no line and no chance of a boat surviving the trip to the ship, the crew and their rescuers were helpless. Some shouted to Squirrel that he should lash himself to the rigging until the tide lowered and they could risk getting him ashore. But he didn't.

It wouldn't have helped.

The passenger aboard the ship, Napier surveyor Henry Skeet, later told an inquest: 'I watched him for a quarter of an hour, and then left him to go and speak with the captain, who was lying exhausted beside a fire. I had just gone away, when Julia [Huria], a Maori woman, said, "The pakeha has let go." I looked round, and [Squirrel] had gone. I went back to the beach near the wreck, to watch in case [he] should come up, but did not see his body till next morning, when it was found upwards of a mile from the wreck.'

Morgan told the inquest: 'If it had not been for the Maoris, not one of us would have been saved. Neither boat, canoe nor ship could live in such a gale and such a sea.'

The inquest concluded that Squirrel's death was an accidental drowning, and the jury recommended that the heroic deeds of their rescuers deserved hearty public gratitude.

Two months later, Huria and Hemi Matenga and Hohapeta Kahupuku (also known as Ropata) were each presented with £50 by the people of Nelson and the government. Two others received £10 each for assisting the shipwrecked men after they'd reached the shore.

A Mr H.J. Goodman, of a Nelson settlers' committee, also presented Huria with a gold watch and chain, and her kinsmen with silver watches and chains. To Huria, he said: 'Your heroism is acknowledged by others, not only here, but in far-off places; and it is our pride that Nelson possesses a woman capable of showing such bravery.'

To loud cheers, Hemi Matenga—who had also ridden 32 kilometres into Nelson in the hours following the shipwreck to get help for the stranded men—told the gathering he and his family were honoured. 'We had no idea, at the time we saved the Europeans' lives, of receiving any reward. We heard their cry for help, and we assisted them.'

Though Huria Matenga, who received most of the credit for the rescue, became a household name throughout New Zealand, she rarely spoke of her feat. The most she would say is, 'It was nothing,' before changing the subject.

The bay in which the brig was wrecked now takes the ill-fated ship's name: Delaware Bay.

Frank Worsley

Shackleton's saviour

They were the worst pack ice conditions anyone had seen. Almost 2000 kilometres of the stuff lay between Ernest Shackleton's ship the *Endurance* and his destination: Antarctica. He had been warned they would never make it.

From the helm, Akaroa-born captain Frank Worsley marvelled at the great blocks of ice as they rose and fell swiftly and violently all around. Shackleton had hired the spirited 42-year-old sailor just minutes after meeting him in London several months earlier. His instinct was to prove correct; Worsley's freakish navigational skills and stamina would later save the lives of all 28 men on board.

Despite the hazards, Shackleton was determined. Twice already the South Pole had proved elusive to him. With World War I beginning and little hope of getting the funding for another Antarctic expedition, he feared that returning to England would mark the end of his dream.

The famed British explorer had made it as close as 190 kilometres from the South Pole in 1909 but just three years later his effort was trumped when Norwegian explorer Roald Amundsen reached it. With no glory left in merely getting to Earth's southernmost point, Shackleton vowed to go one further–to be the first to cross the entire Antarctic continent on foot.

On 7 December 1914 the *Endurance* arrived at the pack ice that guarded the frozen continent. Before them lay a slowly moving jigsaw puzzle of ice floes, snow-capped icebergs, patches of soupy, mushy ice and pools of open water. They would skirt around the floes until they found a weak patch. If they were lucky they could simply weave through the gaps between the ice. If they weren't they could rear up and smack into it with the purpose-built ship's heavy wooden hull.

Expedition photographer Frank Hurley described the technique in his diary: 'When the ship comes in impact with the ice she stops, dead, shivering from truck to kelson; then almost immediately a long crack starts from our bow, into which we steam, and, like a wedge slowly force the crack sufficiently to enable a passage to be made.'

Worsley, a good-natured daredevil who had served on a steamer in the Canadian Arctic, specialised in ice-ramming. The expedition's chief surgeon, Alexander Macklin, later wrote: 'I have a sneaking suspicion that he often went out of his way to find a nice piece of floe at which he could drive at full speed and cut in two; he loved to feel the shock, the riding up, and the sensation as the ice gave and we drove through.'

For weeks they lived like that. As they inched south, the icebergs grew bigger and the pools narrowed into small channels. It began to look more like a glacier than an ocean. Worsley took to commanding the ship from the crow's nest.

On 10 January they spotted land but Shackleton was determined to keep going south. Every mile on board the ship would save them a mile of dragging their supplies on sledges. Five days later they came to a bay that looked promising but Shackleton decided to press on. For the rest of his life he regretted that decision.

On 18 January a gale whipped up and the *Endurance* was forced to shelter behind an iceberg. The following morning they found themselves wedged in ice, only one day's sail from their destination. Worsley could see no water at all from the crow's nest. Still, they expected that once the gale had subsided the ice would break up again.

Days passed slowly. Occasionally they would spot a patch of water opening up and try to crash through, but it was hopeless. They even climbed out and chipped at the ice with picks, chisels and saws. On 24 February Shackleton declared they would have to winter over on the ship.

The ice continued to move and the ship drifted slowly out of sight of land. As winter set in, so too did boredom. One day, for laughs, Worsley went for a skinny dip. On another he and Shackleton danced a two-step on the ice.

In mid-July a blizzard hit and the temperature plummeted. The ice began to build, grinding against the sides of the ship. The vessel groaned and shuddered under the pressure. Huge frozen blocks started slowly tumbling towards them. Below them the ice was opening and closing as if in an earthquake. The ship was knocked about: forward and backward; side to side. Its beams bulged, its door frames buckled.

Shackleton calculated that the blizzard had shoved them 60 kilometres. He told Worsley it was only a matter of time before they would have to abandon the ship. 'What the ice gets, the ice keeps,' he said.

And still there was nothing to do but wait. Months passed. October came and the ice began to thaw. At one point the *Endurance* even drifted into a patch of water, though it wasn't long before the ice closed in again. Hopes were raised and dashed with cruel regularity. The ship became caught in an icy vice that wound tighter and tighter until, on October 27, it snapped.

Worsley wrote in his diary: 'Pressure throughout the day, increasing to terrific force at 4 p.m., heaving stern up, smashing rudder, rudderpost and sternpost. Decks breaking up. 7 p.m.: Ship too dangerous to live in. We are forced to abandon her. Water overmastering pumps and coming up to engire fires. Draw fires and let down steam. Men and dogs camp on floe but have to shift camp twice with the floe cracking and smashing underfoot. Get little sleep.'

They hastily rescued the ship's supplies and left it to be crushed and eventually swallowed. Shackleton came up with a plan to drag the life boats to the continent, now 500 kilometres away, camping on ice floes along the way. Worsley thought it was a bad idea, but Shackleton prevailed.

After almost two months it was obvious they were getting nowhere. Shortly after Christmas 1915—more than a year since they had arrived at the ice—they made a more permanent camp with their thin linen tents on a particularly solid ice floe. They called it Patience Camp. They ran low on food and began to shoot and eat their sledge dogs. As they slept, the snow underneath them would melt and seep into their sleeping bags. For five months they slowly drifted with the floe.

In early April they spotted an island. It was fortunate timing—the ice underneath them was beginning to crack. One night it opened up under a tent, plunging one man into the water.

They pushed off in their three life boats on April 9, with just their tents strung up to provide cover. The responsibility for navigation rested heavily upon Worsley. 'If there was a mistake in my sights, which were taken under very difficult conditions, 28 men would have sailed out to death,' he later wrote.

For five days they rowed, sailed and drifted through large swells, snowy squalls and almost constant rain. Blocks of ice threatened to hole the boats and they had to be continuously bailed of freezing water. Frost clung to the men's beards and they fought seasickness. At one point they were surrounded by killer whales. Towards the end of their journey the unthinkable happened: the temperature rose and they ran out of ice. Though the thaw had obvious advantages, it also meant they had no more drinking water. Their throats became too dry to swallow food.

'Most of the men were now looking seriously worn and strained,' wrote Shackleton later. 'Their lips were cracked and their eyes and eyelids showed red in their salt-encrusted faces.'

For days Worsley divided his time between steering and attacking the oars. 'We were in the midst of confused lumpy seas running from two directions,' he recalled. 'The boats could never settle down and to steer became a work of art.'

As they neared land he spent eighteen hours straight at the tiller, until his eyes were so cold he could no longer see, his fingers were frostbitten, his clothes were frozen and he was slumping into sleep. When the men insisted on relieving him they had to forcibly straighten him out and rub him down to restore circulation. He slept briefly—for the first time in 90 hours.

But he had brought them to Elephant Island. It was a barren and inhospitable outpost, but at least it wasn't melting, and there were small colonies of birds, seals and penguins to hunt. As they stumbled onto the shore Shackleton congratulated Worsley.

Their relief was tempered by the knowledge that no one would think to look for them there. With winter approaching and ice floes reappearing, Shackleton knew their only hope was to send the largest of the three boats to raise the alarm at a whaling station on the island of South Georgia, a morale-destroying 1300 kilometres away across open ocean. This they would have to do in a seven-metre boat using just a sextant and chronometer for navigation, with no landmarks and with clouds obscuring the sun and stars.

It was a case of risking the lives of a few for a chance to save them all. Shackleton chose six men for the journey. Worsley was number one on his list. His navigational ability and skill with small boats was unsurpassed, he had designed the boat they would be taking: the *James Caird,* and he had become Shackleton's most trusted confidant.

Worsley was comfortable on the sea but he knew Shackleton had no love for it. He offered to take charge of the boat and leave the explorer on the relative safety of the land. But Shackleton was adamant.

Before they'd left the *Endurance*, Worsley had worked out many different courses, including the route from Elephant Island to South Georgia. It was a fortunate act of forethought. Now he couldn't even use the position of the sun and the stars to check his directions—unyielding grey clouds carpeted the skies.

He later detailed what they were up against: 'The great unceasing westerly swell of the Southern Ocean rolls almost unchecked around this end of the world. The highest, broadest and longest swells in the world, rising forty, fifty feet or more from crest to hollow, these blue waters in a very heavy gale move 25 miles an hour and sometimes even 50 or more . . . Many a good ship has foundered with all hands; a tossing lifeboat or a grating alone remaining to mark their grave.'

On 24 April 1916 they set out. The little boat, provisioned with meagre rations, almost capsized going through the breakers. Their only protection from the elements was a small cabin the ship's carpenter had hastily constructed. Its roof was so low they couldn't sit up in it. Their sleeping bags were already beginning to rot and their oilskins and boots had long since disintegrated.

The castaways watched them go, a tiny speck of hope disappearing into murky seas. By the next day the bay had filled with pack ice.

The six crewmen quickly fell into a pattern: at any one time, three men would be trying to sleep, one steering and the other two pumping, bailing, reefing, furling and doing anything else required.

On day two they struck a cross sea that sent the boat tumbling about. The only relief for the crew's seasickness was the icy water that periodically bucketed off the canvas and down their necks, momentarily shocking them out of their nausea.

'We were lifted up and hurled down,' recalled Worsley. 'With her bows and our bodies we whipped, swept, flailed and stamped on the seas. We leaped on the swells, danced on them, flew over them and dived into them. We wagged like a dog's tail, shook like a flag in a gale, and switchbacked over hills and dales. We were sore all over.'

Gale-force winds constantly blew them off course—and sometimes backwards for days. With no stars and no candle to light the compass, night-time navigation was pure guesswork. By daylight it wasn't much better. The sun peeped through the storm-torn clouds only once or twice a week. The boat pitched so wildly that Worsley had to be held down so he didn't go overboard while he concentrated. His navigation books and logs became soaked almost to a pulp. The pages stuck together and were impossible to write in. He had to open them carefully to avoid destroying their only chance at finding land.

He described in his autobiography the challenge of taking observations: 'I peered out from our burrow—precious sextant cuddled under my chest to prevent seas falling on it. Sir Ernest stood by under the canvas with chronometer, pencil and book. I shouted, "Stand by," and knelt on the thwart—two men holding me up on either side. I brought the sun down to where the horizon ought to be and as the boat leaped frantically upward on the crest of a wave, snapped a good guess at the altitude and yelled, "Stop," Sir Ernest took the time and I worked out the result. Then the fun started! Our fingers were so cold that he had to interpret his wobbly figures—my own so illegible that I had to recognise them by feats of memory.'

At dawn on day eight they discovered the boat was covered in heavy ice up to 40 centimetres deep, weighing it perilously low in the water. They took turns to creep out in the storm and attack the ice with an axe, as the sea washed over them.

On day nine they lost their sea anchor. At midnight on day thirteen Shackleton spotted something white towards the horizon. It was the crest of the biggest wave he'd ever seen. He shouted, 'For God's sake, hold on!' The boat was picked up and flung forward into the breaking surf. Miraculously, it stayed upright. 'We baled with the energy of men fighting for life,' said Shackleton.

Worsley calculated the *James Caird* was nearing South Georgia. But with several days still to go they struck another problem: their last keg of drinking water was contaminated. And the ice that had plagued them for so long was gone, just as it could have become useful. The salt water that lashed their faces made their thirst grow into a burning pain.

At midday on 8 May the clouds on the horizon parted to reveal the black cliffs of South Georgia. The hope the sight brought was tempered by a heavy sea and a battering cross wind. By noon the following day the wind had become a hurricane and was pushing them straight for the steep cliffs. They steered, pumped and bailed with all their might. Their sails seemed as useless as handkerchiefs.

Worsley recalled: 'Foot by foot we staggered and lurched drunkenly past the ravening black fangs of the rocky point . . . As we looked at that hellish rock-bound coast, with its roaring breakers, we wondered at which spot our end was to come.'

For nine hours they fought the hurricane, not daring to land, though their tongues were swollen with thirst. The wind suddenly subsidised. The next day they spotted the entrance to a bay. It took four hours of tacking into strong winds, but in the late afternoon they pulled the *James Caird* up onto a beach.

The men were exhausted. They'd barely rested in the 16-day trip. It took an entire day for them to haul the boat to safety, a job that would normally have taken an hour.

And still the ordeal was not over. A check of the sextant confirmed they had been forced to land in King Hakon Bay on the north-western side of the island. The whaling stations were on the other side, over an uncharted 65-kilometre wilderness of icy peaks. They couldn't risk taking the battered boat back out.

Shackleton decided to take two men on the hike over the island while the others camped in a cave. First he asked Worsley, as he was sure of his endurance under strain. 'I squeezed his arm for this,' recalled Worsley, 'for I felt proud and grateful.' He also chose Tom Crean, the *Endurance*'s hardy and trusted second officer.

At 3 a.m. on 19 May, after three days holed up in bad weather, they set out into sludgy ankle-deep snow. Their clothes were little better than rags and they had put screws in the soles of their worn shoes to give them leverage on the ice. They took no sleeping bags; they did not plan to rest. If they got into trouble there would be no escape.

For six hours they struggled through an undulating sheet of snow and ice, at times sinking into snow up to their knees, or roping up and staggering blindly through fog. They narrowly avoided falling into a crevasse in the gloom. They did have some rare luck: the dawn brought sunshine, something they had seen little of for weeks.

After stopping for breakfast, they reached a range of five rocky crags that appeared to offer four possible passes. They picked the closest. It took three hours to climb to the saddle but there was no way down. Worsley felt sickened.

They returned to the base of the crags and picked another possible route. It was a slightly steeper climb, and also proved fruitless. They retreated and tried again. The next climb was even steeper. In the late afternoon, as the sun dropped behind the mountains and the cold seeped into their bones, they came to the saddle. Still there was no possible path, though from their lofty position they could see into the next gap. It looked encouraging.

They retreated again and began climbing. When they reached the ridge they were silent. Before them lay a flank of steep ice that disappeared into fog. 'We've got to take a risk,' said Shackleton.

They began a painstakingly slow descent. In 30 minutes they covered just 100 metres, which brought them to a slope of snow. Shackleton said, 'We'll slide.' They clung together in tandem formation and held on.

'I was never more scared in my life than for the first thirty seconds,' recalled Worsley. 'We seemed to shoot into space. For a moment my hair fairly stood on end. Then quite suddenly I felt a glow, and knew that I was grinning. I was actually enjoying it . . . I yelled with excitement, and found that Shackleton and Crean were yelling too.'

They slid almost two kilometres in a matter of minutes, dropping about 800 metres, then rewarded themselves with dinner. At 7 p.m. the moon rose and they set off again. By midnight they found they were on a long, steady decline. After two hours they approached what looked like a bay. Their mood soared, but as they walked they discovered great crevasses. It wasn't a bay; it was a glacier. They had overshot their mark and had to retrace their steps for several hours.

They found a steep alternative route. Worsley felt wearier than he had in many days, as much from hopelessness as from fatigue. The men trudged silently, each caught up in an inner struggle. They headed for the only opening they could see in a ridge of rocky mountains ahead.

At 6 a.m. they reached the gap and rested. They picked out what looked like their destination. Sure enough, at 7 a.m. they heard the whistle of the whaling station. 'Yoicks!' shouted Worsley. 'Tally ho!'

There was still a steep, slippery descent to navigate. Roped together, they began inching down, cutting steps in the ice as they went. Impatience forced them to take risks but their luck held. After three hours they reached a bay. A plateau and one last ridge lay between them and safety.

Halfway across the plateau Crean shot downwards with a loud crack. He'd fallen waist-deep into icy water. It wasn't a plateau; it was a frozen lake. They fished him out and continued with more care.

By mid-afternoon they stood on the last ridge, looking down into Stromness Bay. A whaling ship sailed into view and people appeared at the station. They slid and staggered for another hour or two. Then they were there. They had made it to the whaling station in 36 hours.

The Norwegian captain of the station had met Shackleton before, but didn't recognise the filthy, bearded figure in his torn clothing.

'Who the hell are you?' he asked, through an interpreter.

'My name is Shackleton.'

A boat was immediately despatched for King Haakon Bay. As it set out, at 9 p.m., a south-east gale set in for the night. Had the trio been caught in it, they would probably have died.

The rest of the *James Crean* crew was picked up, but the rescue of the castaways of Elephant Island was no straightforward task. Three times in the next three months Shackleton, Crean and Worsley sourced a boat and set out. Three times they were forced to retreat—twice because of pack ice, once because of a broken engine. Winter had firmly set in and the three men thought constantly of their crewmates. Worsley watched the lines on Shackleton's face become furrows and his thick, wavy hair develop streaks of grey.

Finally, on 30 August 1916, in a tug steamer they'd begged from the Chilean government, the three men apprehensively approached the bay where they'd left the rest of the crew four cold months earlier. It was two years almost to the day since the expedition had left England.

The pack ice had cleared. As Worsley manoeuvred the boat between icebergs and hidden reefs, Shackleton peered through his binoculars. In strained tones he counted the figures that began to crawl out of the makeship camp. Finally he let out a shout. 'They're all there, skipper! They're all there!'

It took just 45 minutes to load their friends and the few possessions worth saving. First Officer Lionel Greenstreet was first to climb aboard and greet Worsley: 'We knew that it would be all right if you were on board, Skipper . . . you weren't born to be drowned.'

As they prepared to head out, Worsley wrote in his log: '2.10 All well! At last! 2.15 Full speed ahead.'

The men eventually returned to Europe—and the war. Worsley immediately joined the Royal Navy and took command of two Q-ships (anti-submarine ships). In mid-1918 he served under Shackleton on a secret military mission in Russia. He was mentioned in dispatches and in 1920 was appointed an OBE.

Worsley and Shackleton remained close friends. In 1921 they set out together on another Antarctic expedition but four months into it Shackleton had a fatal heart attack in his cabin, as they were moored off South Georgia. He was buried on the island; a black cairn and cross marking his grave.

Worsley went on to serve in World War II with the Red Cross in France and Norway. Legend has it that he was initially given command of a merchant ship in the war but was fired when his bosses discovered he was nearly 70. He died of lung cancer in 1943, just shy of 71.

He received many accolades, both for his Antarctic adventure and his military exploits. Sir Edmund Hillary later praised his 'courage, skill and determination under the most appalling conditions'. But no tribute meant more to him than the reception he'd received from the whalers of South Georgia.

Shortly after Worsley, Crean and Shackleton had arrived at the station, a gnarled, white-haired Norwegian sailor had approached them. He'd told them he'd been at sea for 40 years and had never heard of such a feat of daring seamanship as theirs, capped off with their icy tramp.

He'd finished with a dramatic gesture. 'These are *men*!' he said.

Arthur Bell
Cyril Ellis
John Holman
William Inglis

Tangiwai heroes

It was supposed to be a quiet Christmas Eve for Cyril Ellis. The Taihape postal clerk was planning to spend the night at his parents' house at Rangataua, near Okahune, with his wife and mother-in-law. But near the end of their 50 kilometre drive north, the 27-year-old suddenly stopped his truck. The road ahead and the bridge in the distance—over the usually shallow Whangaehu River at Tangiwai—was submerged under a roaring yellow torrent.

It was a curious sight, given that it was a clear night and there had been no rain to speak of for several days. In fact, it was a freak lahar that had been unleashed from Mt Ruapehu's crater lake hours earlier and had tumbled down the river, carrying with it a tsunami of 340,000 cubic metres of water, huge blocks of ice, volcanic rubble, sand, silt and boulders.

Ellis backed the truck to a safe spot, grabbed a torch and went for a closer look. It was then he saw a strong light approaching from the south. He called out to his wife to say that a car was coming, but no sooner had he spoken than he realised it wasn't a car. It was a train. And he knew that if the road bridge was covered by water, the train would have no hope of getting across the railway bridge upstream.

On the other side of the river, Arthur Bell, who'd been on his way to Waiouru with his wife, had also stopped his car. Through the darkness he could hear a deafening roar, and within it the thumping of boulders. Then he too saw the train approaching. For the moment he and his wife could do nothing but watch.

Ellis, who was at least on the same side as the train, followed his instinct. 'I jumped the railway fence and ran up the embankment,' he told the *New Zealand Herald* the following day. 'I ran down the middle of the track, brandishing my torch and shouting at the top of my voice in an endeavour to attract the attention of the engine driver or fireman. I ran away from the bridge to try and give the crew more room to pull the train up, but it was no use—they just didn't see the torch. I jumped clear and yelled to the driver when the locomotive roared past me about 200 yards from the bridge, but he had no chance of hearing me above the roar of both the river and engine.'

On board the train, guard William Inglis was sitting in the guard's van at the rear. With the train brimming with 285 people travelling from Wellington to Auckland for Christmas, their gifts stuffed into every spare spot, it was a busy night. The train passed through Tangiwai Station at 10.20 p.m. About two minutes later the brakes were slammed on and Inglis was thrown forward and then backward. There were two more jolts, then the van abruptly stopped. Inglis knew what that meant—either a hose had burst or the train carriages had somehow separated.

Seconds after the engine had passed Ellis, it had reached the bridge. Though both Bell and Ellis knew the road bridge was submerged, what they couldn't see in the darkness was that the pressure of the rocks and water had actually swept most of the 80-metre-long railway bridge and two of its heavy concrete supports into the torrent. The engine and the first few carriages hit nothing but air—and then water.

'The train went straight on over the bridge,' recalled Ellis. 'Halfway across, the engine simply nose-dived off the southern bank and seemed to go, with a bellowing splash nearly against the opposite bank. The first carriage went with it. You never heard such a noise. It sounded as if the engine had exploded. The second carriage reared up, nose first, and, with the weight of the carriages behind it, was more or less catapulted into the air.'

Ellis watched as three more carriages hit the water. They were carried downstream with their lights still on and then disappeared into the night. One carriage was left teetering on the edge of the remaining track, at a 45 degree angle, still attached to the last carriage and Inglis' guard's van.

As the stunned guard climbed down from the van, Ellis sprinted towards him, his torch waving. He yelled, 'For heaven's sake, get the people out of that front carriage.' As he reached Inglis, he said, 'I tried to stop him [the driver]. But he was going too fast. Half your train is in the river.'

'No!' the guard exclaimed in disbelief.

'It is, it is,' yelled Ellis.

Inglis climbed into the teetering carriage, followed by Ellis. Through an open door at one end he could see a metre or two of track stretching out into space, and the river gushing less than two metres below. 'Good God,' he said. 'There is an engine and five cars in there.'

There were still 22 passengers in the carriage, plus Ellis and the guard. Inglis urged them to hurry to the carriage's rear doors. But as he stood in the centre of the car he felt it begin to rock, slightly at first, then more violently. The front of it began to tilt downwards. He clung to the luggage rack. A few passengers screamed.

‘Don’t panic,’ he shouted. ‘Hang on to the luggage racks.’

As the carriage rocked and bounced, he could hear the water rushing nearer. The lights went out, the coupling cracked, he felt an almighty bump and the carriage tipped on to its side. Inglis realised they were being swept downstream. Water surged through the carriage with such force that many passengers’ clothes were ripped from them, and they were pummelled with their own luggage. To Ellis, who had also gone down with the carriage, it felt as if they were spinning in a barrel of water.

The carriage came to a stop, resting precariously on its side against a bank 55 metres downstream of the bridge. The icy water—mixed with mud and oil—was swirling through the carriage. It was up to shoulder height, and rising. There was only a 30 centimetre gap between the water and the side of the train, which had effectively become its roof. A couple of women were clinging to Ellis, whose torch was still shining. Thinking quickly, he knocked out a window with his elbow, then kicked out the glass.

He heard a voice: ‘Can you get my wife out?’ It was John Holman, a printer from Wellington.

‘Righto sport,’ said Ellis. He climbed out the window and Holman hoisted his wife, Delia, up to him. One by one Holman fished out passengers and lifted them to Ellis, who jumped back on to a seat inside so he could more easily guide them out the window. At one point, Holman resorted to biting a man to shock him into moving. Inglis, meanwhile, was helping passengers climb through other smashed windows. It took only a few minutes for the men to clear the carriage.

Even as they were making their escape, the surge was passing. By the time Inglis emerged, the water near the bank was only knee-deep. A group of passersby and local men who’d rushed in to help formed a human chain through the river to guide the passengers to safety. The train’s engine lay in the water nearby, ‘puffing and hissing like some monster caught in a trap', according to the account of survivor Joan Karam.

Meanwhile, on the opposite bank, Arthur Bell and his wife had sprung into action. As soon as they'd realised what was happening, his wife had turned the car around and sped away to get help.

Bell then scrambled down the riverbank to one of the stricken carriages. He grabbed a man who'd managed to escape the wreckage but was having trouble standing in the current, and hauled him to safety. Then he waded to the carriage, smashed the windows, and began to pull people out and guide them to firm ground. Though the river level had receded, the churning mixture of water, debris, silt and oil was still gushing by with such force that it was a struggle for Bell to get even the lightest of the passengers to the bank. Most of them were injured, which made moving them even more difficult.

Of the 285 people who were on that train on 24 December 1953, 151 died, including the driver, Charles Parker. Six of its seven carriages and the engine had plunged into the river. The force of the water was so great that the fifth carriage was swept 2.5 kilometres downstream.

But in the sixth and last carriage to be swept away, only one passenger died—a young woman who'd become trapped under a seat, her head below the gushing waters. Ellis, Inglis and Holman were credited with saving the carriage's 21 other passengers. On the other bank of the river, Arthur Bell had pulled about 15 people to safety.

All four men received bravery awards from the Queen, who was visiting New Zealand that Christmas. Cyril Ellis and John Holman received the George Medal, awarded for civilian acts of bravery, and William Inglis and Arthur Bell won the British Empire Medal for gallantry.

'I can't explain what we went through,' said Ellis later, 'but somehow in the stress of the moment both John [Holman] and I seemed to have terrific strength.'

William Galloway
Alan Pain
John Ross
Alun Williams

Wahine rescuers

Alun Williams was impatient. It was early afternoon on 10 April 1968 and the ferry *Wahine* and her 734 passengers and crew were in danger. Early that morning the ship had been swept off course by cyclone Giselle and had struck a reef near the entrance to Wellington Harbour. It was now listing in high seas, its engines destroyed. The order had come to abandon ship and, with many of its life rafts unable to be launched or rendered useless by the stormy conditions, hundreds of passengers had been left with no choice but to jump straight into the churning water.

Williams, a burly Welsh fireman working at Wellington Airport, had tried to launch a rubber Zodiac boat from Seatoun Beach to join the rescue effort, but it had been swamped by one of the huge waves pounding the coastline.

He couldn't bear to wait while his boss and workmates bailed it out and checked the motor. He threw a life raft into a nearby private cruiser, the *Maru*, which was setting out on its own rescue mission, with Miramar fireman Peter Webster at the helm. Williams leapt aboard, along with another airport fireman, Malcolm Yates.

Meanwhile, in heavy swells out on the edge of the breaking sea, the Wellington Harbour Board tugboat *Taioma* was picking up passengers and crew from three *Wahine* life rafts. On one of the rafts was the ferry's pantryman, John Ross, the father of three young children. As his little vessel came alongside the tugboat, he steadied it by grabbing a cargo net slung from the larger boat.

One by one the occupants of the raft clambered into the boat, until only two people were left: Ross and a young woman. But the terrified woman refused to let go of the raft and climb up to a spot from where she could be hauled aboard.

The tug was in a precarious position. Its intakes were drawing in sand and kelp and it was in danger of grounding. It could wait no longer. Someone shouted to Ross to climb aboard but he refused. 'I'm OK,' he said. 'I'll look after her.' Ross, who had no life jacket, let go of the net and the raft drifted away into the gloom. The tug had no option but to leave the pair to fate.

On board the ailing ferry, deputy harbour master William Galloway and skipper Captain Hector Robertson were checking for any remaining passengers. The vessel was listing heavily to starboard, much of its furniture and fittings broken by the storm. Amid the chaos, it was spookily quiet.

Galloway raced through the accommodation on B deck, shouting, 'Is anybody there?' There was no answer. In fact, all of the 610 passengers and 120 of the crew had left the ship in just half an hour, leaving just Galloway, Robertson and two crew members. Once the captain was satisfied the ship was empty, the two crew members jumped into the water. There were no lifeboats left. Wearing life jackets, they were at the mercy of the sea.

The captain turned to Galloway. 'All right, Bill, it's your turn now.' Galloway jumped, followed by Robertson. It was 2.10 p.m., seven-and-a-half hours after the ship had run aground on Barrett

Reef. It had lost its starboard propeller and motor, followed by its port motor, and water had swamped its vehicle deck and destabilised it. The weather was so wild that day that a crewman who'd crawled out to help drop an anchor from the forecastle, to stop the ship drifting into rocks, had been picked up by the wind, hurled through the air and flung against the ship's railings.

Galloway hadn't been on the ship for its overnight journey from Lyttelton. He'd leaped aboard in Wellington Harbour at midday from the harbour board's pilot launch, *Tiakina*, after a failed attempt by the tugboat *Tapuhi* to tow the ferry to deeper waters. The launch was at that point being lifted six to ten metres in the swell and the winds were of hurricane force. Galloway had waited until the *Tiakina* was within range of the swinging ferry, then jumped from her to a lifeboat ladder on the bigger vessel.

A report by a court of investigation noted later: '*Tiakina* stood by *Wahine*, then sheered towards her, and Captain Galloway seized his opportunity to jump on to one of the lifeboat ladders hanging over *Wahine*'s starboard side, and then to clamber up on to her deck. He passed over this lightly in his evidence, but the fact remains that the feat called for great personal courage as well as skill . . . [It] involved the acceptance by Captain Galloway of great risk to life, apart altogether from outstanding agility and seamanship.'

The danger had not passed for Galloway once he'd caught the ladder. It was still a ten-metre climb to the boat deck, and at one point he'd slid downwards and was lucky not to be crushed between the two boats.

Robertson, who'd watched from the bridge, later recalled: 'He slipped down a couple of rungs and I thought he was going to be chopped in two by the launch when it came back and hit us.'

Once on deck, Galloway had barely given himself time to catch his breath. He'd immediately made his way to the wheelhouse to offer his help to Robertson. The captain was at last able to hand the wheel over while he inspected the ship and decided the next step. By 12.45 p.m. the helpless vessel was leaning to starboard, swinging from five to 25 degrees. Shortly before 1.20 p.m. Galloway had realised that the ship just didn't feel right and, sure enough, it suddenly swung to port, putting it at risk of capsizing in the combination of strong seas, fierce winds and ebbing tide.

Galloway and Robertson had then made the call to abandon ship. At 1.25 p.m. Galloway had radioed the decision to the Beacon Hill signal station on shore and told the tug *Tapuhi* to stand by to rescue passengers. It would be about 35 minutes—after everyone but the captain was off the ship—before he followed his own orders.

Once they jumped overboard, Galloway and Robertson spent at least 30 minutes in the rolling seas before being picked up by a private launch. Within minutes of their rescue the *Wahine* heaved right over onto her starboard side with a great puff of yellow steam. If they'd given the order to abandon ship any later, passengers would have been trapped inside.

When Alun Williams and his colleagues reached the ship it had settled horizontally on the sea bed. Williams could see about 25 people dotted in turbulent water to the east. Getting to them wasn't going to be easy.

'We'd try to pull alongside someone in the trough of a wave, only to find another twenty-footer come thundering down on us,' helmsman Peter Webster later recalled. 'We had to leave whoever we were attempting to pick up, open up the throttle and try again. We were close to foundering three or four times and rode over a couple of the large waves side on. Luckily we didn't ship much water. The boat would have been in real trouble if the sea had doused the exposed engine.'

Given the conditions it was proving impossible to get anyone up into the launch, so Webster had to make the difficult decision to retreat to calmer waters. But Williams wasn't about to give up. As

Webster and Yates struggled to keep the boat from being swamped, Williams heaved his life raft over the side, inflating it as he did so. He then jumped into the water beside it. As Webster and Yates reluctantly turned the boat around, Williams clambered aboard the raft then, with the lifeline secured to his body, dived off and swam out into the murky waters towards the exhausted survivors.

Later, Williams told it like this: 'I took the lifeline and went back into the water, going round and pulling people into the raft.'

But in their book *The Wahine Disaster*, journalists Max Lambert and Jim Hartley wrote: 'There was a good deal more to it than that. He swam through the turmoil of the sea to the half-drowned survivors, tugging and pushing them towards the life raft. Getting the first couple aboard called for a tremendous effort; heaving them from the water up and over the slippery, smooth sides of the raft as it jumped up and down.'

Williams made many trips between the boat and the survivors, the lifeline trailing behind him. The overalls he was wearing had a built-in life jacket but he didn't inflate it, figuring it would slow him down and lessen his chances of saving people. He rescued six people and retrieved one body. The others he'd seen in the water had, by that time, drifted too far away to be helped. He climbed back on the raft, turned it to shore and landed it safely on the rocky coastline.

Meanwhile, a flotilla of private boats had joined the rescue effort. One was the *Nereides*, a 13-metre 42-year-old wooden launch crewed by Lower Hutt businessman Allan Pain, housewife Joan Ward and her twelve-year-old son Peter.

The slow old boat was one of the last to join the rescue. With other vessels picking up survivors around Eastbourne, Pain decided to head south to Pencarrow Head. Only as he neared the head did he realise how fierce the conditions were. The incoming swell and the outgoing tide were churned into a maelstrom. Peter later remembered the waves to be nine to twelve metres high and starting to break.

'There we were,' recalled his mother, 'a man, a housewife and a schoolboy in the middle of these wild seas. None of us was prepared for that.'

Pain quickly discovered that the risk had been worth it. He spotted three people being tossed violently in the water. They were clinging to a single lifebuoy and were drifting towards wave-churned rocks on the Pencarrow coastline. Dead bodies were visible along that stretch of coast.

The tugboat *Tapuhi* had earlier tried to rescue the trio, along with several others, but had been forced to abandon them because of the massive waves. Its crew had thrown them the lifebuoy.

One of the three was student Kathryn Dallas. 'Huge breakers were hurtling towards us and breaking over us in white water,' she later remembered. 'Water kept washing into my nose and mouth. I could scarcely gasp.'

Convinced no one would find them that far out, Dallas was close to giving up hope. But then she spotted a mast. It was the *Nereides*.

The three people on board were, by now, petrified. 'I know I wanted to run away and I think Allan did,' said Ward later, 'but we just couldn't. Allan was scared for us, but he also knew those people were going to die if we didn't help them.'

It was by no means a straightforward manoeuvre. The *Nereides* had high sides, which was going to make it difficult to pull the trio on board, even if they could get close enough without being swamped or smashed into a rock. Pain had to circle the passengers several times. The three swimmers quickly realised their best chance was to abandon the buoy and swim out to the boat.

Ward took the helm while Pain and her son leaned down and dragged aboard the first of the three, Whangarei 16-year-old Paul Field. He slumped onto the deck, alive but barely able to move from exhaustion.

Next it was Dallas' turn, but they struggled. She was weighed down by heavy clothes and the boat was perilously close to the rocks. It had become so shallow that Peter could see the sea bed under them. Great wads of kelp threatened to jam the propeller.

Pain made a desperate decision. He hooked ropes under the arms of Dallas and the third passenger, Cambridge man Brian Townend, and revved up the motor, dragging them to a safe distance. Dallas was screaming with pain. Ward again took the wheel and, with the help of a boat hook, and with Peter leaning perilously over the side, the young woman was dragged aboard.

By this time the airport fireman Alun Williams and his passengers had scrambled ashore. But Williams wasn't out of the water for long. He immediately charged back in and grabbed several people who'd been thrown from a *Wahine* raft as it foundered in the thunderous surf. He helped them to shore then swam out to three others who were 20 metres out. He brought them back one by one but, as he was returning for the third time, he was picked up by a strong wave and pounded onto a rock. The impact cracked a bone at the base of his spine and left him with internal bruising.

He made it to the beach, where he draped his life jacket over an exhausted woman in an effort to keep her warm. He left her in the care of several police officers and walked barefoot along the coast to an unofficial mustering point. 'It was bloody grim,' he said later. He was reported safe at 4.37 p.m., nearly four hours after he'd set out from his base at the airport.

Back out at the heads, Brian Townend, still tied alongside the *Nereides*, was starting to fade. Ward, relieved of the wheel, could do little but reach down and hold his hand, powerless to lift him aboard as waves pummelled him. As they struggled, a Zodiac appeared, almost from nowhere. Two harbour board divers in wetsuits leapt into the sea while a third man jumped onto the *Nereides*. Between them they hauled Townend aboard.

Townend is believed to have been the last of the *Wahine* survivors to be plucked out of the sea, but there was little his rescuers could do for him. The 53-year-old former seaman died on deck within minutes, possibly from a heart attack. He had been in the water for three and a half hours.

He was the 51st–and last–person to die that day. Pantryman John Ross was also among the dead. It's not known exactly what happened to Ross after he let his life raft drift away from the *Taioma*, or the panicking passenger he'd stayed to help. The court of inquiry commended his gallantry.

There were many more courageous acts that day. In all, 683 people survived the sinking. Without the efforts of the dozens of police, firefighters, harbour board staff, surf lifesavers, crew, passengers, boaties and others who joined the rescue mission, many of them would also have died.

The court of inquiry report states: 'There is no doubt that on 10 April there were a great many instances of gallantry, courage and even heroism. It is extraordinarily difficult to record details without having the uneasy feeling that other people whose desserts are great will be overlooked.'

Curiously, no medals for bravery were awarded for the heroic exploits of that day. Another of the *Wahine* heroes, former Olympic rower John Gibbons, later told journalist David Lomas that he wondered if doing so would have highlighted the failings of the official rescue.

Said Lomas: 'Heroic action by small boaties, first at Seatoun and later off Eastbourne, saved many lives, but the cockleshell heroes initially went to sea in defiance of authorities . . . neither the police nor the harbour board set in place any serious contingency plan for the *Wahine* sinking, and both were clearly caught unawares when the decision was made to abandon ship.'

Royd Kennedy

Human shield

Before the words left his mouth, Royd Kennedy figured his number was up. Lying beside 12-year-old Shirley Young, her severely burned body pinned beneath the crushing weight of a tandem-axle trailer engulfed in a raging inferno, he promised he would not leave her side.

The senior fire fighter knew it could only be seconds before the 20,000 litres of high-octane fuel in the main tanker exploded into a billowing fireball, killing them both. He took off his helmet, placed it on the little girl's head and strapped it tight, closing the visor over her face. At least she would still be pretty when they pulled her from the wreckage. Then he wrapped her in his arms, shielding her with his body, and prepared to die.

It was 9 August 1990, his wife Rosemary Kennedy's 36th birthday, and earlier that day her mother Joyce had arrived with a cake. She and Rosemary's father had driven up from the Waikato to spend a few days with the Kennedys and their three children at their home in rural Riverhead, west Auckland.

After enjoying a birthday tea, Royd Kennedy climbed onto his beloved 1988 Harley Davidson motorcycle for the 40-minute ride to the Manukau fire station. Hitting the motorway, Kennedy opened up the throttle and moved into the fast lane, relishing the sense of freedom of his regular commute.

Kennedy pulled off the motorway at the off-ramp near the

Manukau City Shopping Centre, then New Zealand's largest mall. It was a Thursday, late-night shopping day and pay day for many of the city's residents. The car park was already starting to fill up.

The station was right next to the motorway and crews were often called to attend high-speed head-on collisions on the notoriously dangerous highway south of Auckland. Kennedy had been stationed at Manukau for less than a year, but he was close to his workmates. Many of them had known each other for years; Kennedy had even trained with two of them as rookies back in 1979. The guys looked out for each other; they understood. Kennedy called it a brotherhood.

Just like brothers, there was plenty of good-natured ribbing that night, as the twelve men of Blue Watch set about cleaning and checking their gear. After parade and inspection, they moved on to the appliances, cab doors slamming, crews chatting as they checked every piece of equipment.

At 7.25 p.m. the men had almost finished a workout in the gym when the alarm sounded the first turn-out of the evening. Two crews were called to a motor vehicle accident on Wiri Station Road, just one kilometre north of the station. It was car versus petrol tanker–and the tanker was on fire.

The men ran to the engine bay, pulling on boots, over-trousers and coats as they went. Through the open doors they could see the glow of the fire against the new ten-storey Manukau City Council building and a thick black column of smoke rising into the cold night air.

The crews scrambled into position, the men helping each other with their gear as the trucks roared into the night, sirens blaring. On board appliance 301, Kennedy attached his breathing apparatus and switched focus, thinking only of the job ahead.

In seconds they had arrived at the scene and the men fell silent, awestruck by the mighty inferno.

This is how Kennedy describes it in his autobiography: 'The whole night sky above Manukau City was lit up as if by a false dawn from this mega-huge, bomb-like fire. The sheer size and power of the explosions was stunning, a thing of shocking beauty. It was magnificent, a giant, and we had to knock the bastard out.

'The mall was about 100 metres from the fire and the crowded car park right next to it. We couldn't see it, but somewhere in the inferno was a petrol tanker and trailer, loaded with more than 36,000 litres of high-octane fuel, source of the all-too-visible liquid fire, the river of flaming petrol which was gushing down a gutter and entering a drain grille, feeding into the massive stormwater system under the shopping centre.

'The petrol, we could see, was threatening to overflow the drain and pour into an adjacent access lane, 30 metres away, leading straight into the mall itself. And it was possible that if enough fuel and vapours escaped at once to mix with the air, the fireball would extend for hundreds of metres.

'The giant flames continued to throw themselves 100 metres into the night sky, the smoke and the heated air above them lost in the darkness. The mere radiating heat would spread fires to surrounding exposures if left unchecked. And we were expected to check it.

'And now, there in the flame, there, the tanker. The trailer section is lying on its side, and is creating the fireball totally enveloping everything including the car and the big mother tanker where there is much more fuel—as yet unexploded. Holy shit, when that goes up—it could be any second.'

Senior station officer John Hyland was in charge of the scene, but until back-up arrived there was little the eight firefighters could do to contain the blaze. Hyland directed his men to lay a blanket of foam on the flaming fuel pouring into the drains, quickly assessing that this posed the greatest threat to the thousands of shoppers in the mall.

The heat was unlike anything Kennedy had known. He could feel it rising through his thick rubber boots and the smallest movement of skin against clothing brought immediate pain. Jets of water evaporated before reaching the target, asphalt steamed, metal boomed and hissed as it twisted and buckled. As each section of the tanker exploded into a fireball, heatwaves radiated outwards, driving the firefighters back.

In the car park, station officer Graham Haycock was attending to the driver of the car, Gaylene Young. She was badly burned and lying on the ground, her clothes burned off. 'My baby . . . ' she cried.

Haycock squinted at the blaze. It seemed impossible that anyone could survive. 'The front bumper of a Ford Cortina car was just visible in the fireball,' recalled Kennedy, 'and the underside of the tanker trailer became visible in the flames and smoke as the rising super-hot air dragged frost-tinged cooler air in at its base like a miniature nuclear mushroom.'

As the two men walked out of the car park, they heard a small voice crying out. Underneath the chassis a tiny hand was waving. 'Cover me Graham!' Kennedy yelled, keeping low as he scuttled towards the trailer and crawled beneath the billowing inferno to where the girl lay badly injured. Shirley Young was pinned beneath the wheels of the truck from the waist down, unable to sit up or lie flat, one leg burning. She clung to Kennedy, screaming for him to help.

'Hello little one' he yelled through the thundering flames. 'My name is Royd and I'm gonna get you out of here.'

Kennedy didn't know whether Haycock had seen him go under the trailer. He didn't know whether anyone could hear him. He couldn't see anything but the child, the trailer and the flames that flashed intermittently through the undercarriage. As he unstrapped his breathing apparatus and propped it under her for support, the stench of petrol was intense. The kid didn't have a chance. This was it.

Flames whooshed over them, searing Shirley's face and burning the hair from the left side of her head. They were both screaming and panicking as Shirley begged Kennedy not to leave her.

Kennedy heard himself say, 'I promise I'll never leave you. But you've got to look after me, Shirley, I'm scared too. It's a bit rough, but we're gonna make it, Shirley, we will, you'll see.'

He was lying. He was confident they were goners.

For Kennedy, there was never any option to back out. 'Once I had seen her hand, I was committed. Once the action was taken, I was locked in. To leave was unthinkable, unforgivable. I wouldn't have been able to live with myself if I had left the child.'

Kennedy kept talking to Shirley as he placed his helmet over her head. He prayed aloud as he hugged her to him, trying to protect her body from the inevitable explosion. He held her arms with his gloved hands, feeling her charred skin gather at the wrists.

And then, calm. 'There was no more panic, just an all-pervading peace. My patchy breaths of fright gave way to a sigh of freedom, and I knew there was a time, and this was mine. So, this was "it". What an extraordinary feeling of ultimate freedom and relaxation. Flying without moving.'

Kennedy lay there talking to Shirley, calming her fears, reassuring her that he wouldn't leave. Waiting to die.

Suddenly a torrent of freezing water rushed into their tiny refuge, 15 litres per second blasting the flames away from the pair. The crews had moved to an extremely dangerous position, withstanding incredible radiated heat and suffering burns through their protective clothing as they fought to save Kennedy and Shirley.

Divisional officer Ray Warby appeared at the edge of the trailer, asking Kennedy for his assessment of the situation. Shirley was in excruciating pain and going into shock and hypothermia from the cold water. They had to get her out, fast. But to do that, they would have to raise the trailer.

Back-up crews arrived, training more water and foam on the trailer. They were both shaking violently now, but Kennedy kept on talking. Cradling her head against his chest, scrambling for something to say, he asked her if she'd ever been horse riding. When she said no, Kennedy asked whether she would like to come and ride his daughter's horse when they got out of there. 'She reckoned that would be really neat,' he recalled.

The crew were trying to stabilise the trailer so they could slide airbags underneath and inflate them enough to raise the wheelbase, sliding Shirley out. But Shirley was fading, her pulse was dropping. She stopped breathing. Kennedy had to scream for a resuscitator, and began desperately pumping air into her lungs.

Shirley opened her eyes. 'If I don't make it, tell Mum I love her.'

'You can tell her yourself,' Kennedy replied. 'We'll soon have you out of here.'

Kennedy kept talking to Shirley, telling her to stay with him, to stay awake.

The airbags weren't enough; Warby had to bring in hydraulic rams to raise the trailer higher. It would be another 20 minutes before the chassis finally began to lift, little by little.

Finally, Kennedy was able to reach down and untangle Shirley's legs. He carefully climbed out from under the trailer, pulling her with him. They'd been huddled together beneath the flaming trailer for an hour. 'We made it,' he said in her ear, as she let go and slipped unconscious on the ambulance stretcher.

Before the shift was over, Kennedy and Haycock had been photographed and interviewed by newspapers and radio stations from all over the country. When Kennedy finally arrived home a television crew was waiting on the doorstep.

Letters of thanks addressed to Kennedy came from all over the world, from MPs and former prime ministers, organisations and schools. Soon the awards began to flow: the *Dominion* newspaper named him Man of the Year and Governor-General Catherine Tizard presented him with the Charles Upham Award for bravery. The chief fire officer from Louisville Fire Department in Kentucky travelled to New Zealand to present him with a Certificate of Valor and he received a Citation of Commendation from the Association of Fire Chiefs of America. Finally, he received notice that Queen Elizabeth II had awarded him the George Medal, the second-highest civilian honour for bravery, following nominations from parliament and the public.

Shirley Young suffered extensive burns and her right leg was amputated just below the knee. Her mother, Gaylene, also survived. Six months after the fire, the Young family visited Kennedy's home and Shirley went riding on their horse, Gilly. 'It was,' wrote Kennedy, 'a very special and emotional day.'

Even then, months after the fire, media attention continued to grow as the story appeared in *Reader's Digest*, on television documentaries and the American television show *Rescue 911*, which included a dramatic reconstruction in which many of the crew played themselves.

Kennedy insists he always maintained the rescue was a joint effort—his colleagues risked their lives to rescue the pair from the blazing trailer. But as media and public attention continued to focus on Kennedy, relations with his colleagues in the Fire Service became strained. Kennedy said he was branded 'Hero Boy' and 'Glory Hunter', that colleagues refused to speak to him and claimed he'd received special treatment.

In the mid-1990s Kennedy was once again in the spotlight when he backed aspects of controversial proposed reforms to the Fire Service. 'I was labelled a scab, a traitor and a turncoat,' he told *New Idea* in 2007. 'I got sent a bullet in the mail.'

Kennedy left the Fire Service in 1997 and moved to Australia. In 2007, he was reunited with Shirley Young and her two small children on a television show, in a moment he described as 'supreme'.

He told the *Dominion Post* it had been his job to put his life on the line for Shirley. 'If you wear that uniform, I expect people to do what I did. I know it's a hard thing to say, but I expect someone to lay their life on the line.'

Jacinda Amey
John Funnell

Remote rescuers

The water was jarringly cold. At barely seven degrees Celsius, it could kill a man within an hour.

The five residents of the sub-Antarctic Campbell Island weren't the type to take chances. The Department of Conservation workers were the only people on a speck of windswept land 600 kilometres south of New Zealand. If they got into trouble it was a three-day boat ride to civilisation.

When they took a break to go snorkelling and body surfing on 24 April 1992 they took the precaution of wearing thick neoprene wetsuits from head to foot. Mike Fraser, the team leader, slipped into the water first. He kicked through towers of swaying kelp and became engrossed in the underwater scenery.

They gradually drifted out into the deeper waters of Northwest Bay, taking advantage of the unusually calm water. Fraser, a dive instructor and underwater photographer, decided to swim to a nearby reef. At that time of the year there was a good chance he would spot a southern right whale.

Researcher Jacinda Amey had been following Fraser but suddenly she stopped. A feeling of unease gripped her. Spooked, she headed back towards the shore.

Fraser was floating on the surface of the water about 30 metres out when an unseen force ploughed into his side. He was wrenched deep into the water, his arms pinned down. Then he surged up again and broke the surface.

He found himself eye to eye with a great white shark. Its teeth had sunk into both his arms, through the wetsuit, through skin, muscle and tissue and into the bone. As the shark tossed him through the water, Fraser tore his left arm free and started bashing the creature as he pushed hard with his knees. 'Shark!' he yelled. 'Shark!'

Near the shore, the others heard a muffled shout. They turned to see Fraser thrashing in the waves. They couldn't make out what he was saying. Amey's first thought was that he was being attacked by a sea lion. She started swimming towards him. Then she watched as he was lifted out of the water, clamped in a pair of enormous jaws. They plunged out of sight.

The first instinct of all his colleagues was to get out of the water. But Amey hesitated. And then she kept swimming–towards Fraser and the shark.

Meanwhile, with an inhuman effort, Fraser shoved the shark off, tearing off his right arm below the elbow. The animal flicked around and disappeared.

Amey swam towards the swarm of blood. She calculated the risks: she knew if she became coated in blood she too could be attacked, leaving them both incapacitated. Fraser weakly reached out to her, managing to get clear of the blood. The petite woman grabbed the much larger man and towed him to shore.

Their colleagues stepped in. Using a first-aid kit from a nearby hut, they stemmed the blood flow from Fraser's arms, applied tourniquets and warmed his body. He had lost half his blood and his breathing was laboured. Fearful of moving him, they erected a tent on the beach.

They sent an emergency message out on a VHF radio but there was no immediate reply. They would need to get to the radio in the main hut. Gus McAllister, the fastest runner among them, set out across the island to make the call.

As night set in, reinforcements arrived: the six crew members of New Zealand fisheries vessel *Tangaroa* were within motoring distance when they heard the call for help. They navigated between the rocks of the uncharted bay in darkness. With Fraser's teammates doing as much as was possible to help him, there was little the crew could do but provide moral support.

Fraser's chances did not look good. He was unlikely to survive a boat journey to the mainland. No one had ever flown in or out of the island and, anyway, there was no airstrip. It would be impossible for a helicopter to fly down from New Zealand—the distance was just too great.

Back in New Zealand, veteran Taupo helicopter pilot John Funnell was in a more optimistic frame of mind. It was 6 p.m. when he was notified of Fraser's predicament. By that time the injured man had been lying on the beach for almost three hours.

No one had ever taken a single-engine helicopter across such a vast distance without stopping. Once they were out of sight of Stewart Island there would be nothing but sea until they got to the sub-Antarctic islands—and then of course they would have to fly straight back.

But Funnell was a pioneer of rescue helicopter services in New Zealand, and he had a Squirrel machine that was capable of flying longer distances than the average rescue chopper. He was prepared to take the risk. So were his co-pilot, Grant Biel, and paramedic Pat Wynne.

As darkness set in, they packed their gear into the helicopter and lifted off.

Just a few hours into the flight the helicopter's GPS (Global Positioning System) went blank. The system had been taken offline for repositioning. Biel, the navigator, had to fall back on his skills in dead reckoning—estimating their position according to their direction and speed. After two hours of flying blind, the little screen flashed back into life.

The helicopter reached the island before dawn. The boat crew, using radar and parachute flares, helped to guide it through the clouds to a patch of grass above the beach. Wynne got to work stabilising Fraser and pumping him with blood before the long flight to Invercargill Hospital.

Fraser made a remarkable recovery thanks to the actions of Amey and his other colleagues, Funnell and his crew and the crew of the research ship. 'I thought my number was up . . . I just owe so much to all of them,' he said later.

For his part in the rescue, Funnell received the New Zealand Bravery Medal. His citation concludes:

'The Squirrel touched down again at Taupo 25 hours after the request to make the trip. The flight over some 1200 kilometres of ocean was believed to be unprecedented anywhere in the world in terms of single-engine helicopter operations and was undertaken at considerable risk to those on board. Mr Funnell displayed bravery in undertaking this flight, without which the shark attack victim would not have survived.'

Amey received New Zealand's highest bravery honour, the New Zealand Cross, for 'great courage and bravery with complete disregard for her own safety'. She is one of just two recipients of the award since its inception in the 1990s.

On the rare occasions the Hamilton-born woman has talked publicly about the rescue, she has emphasised that it was a team effort.

'An occasion like that demonstrated what you can really do when you pull together.'

Brian Pickering

Mountain rescuer

On 25 September 2000 a weather bomb dropped on the Kaimanawa Forest Park. As two imploding fronts battered against each other, conditions rapidly deteriorated into a 50-year storm, bringing unexpected blizzard conditions to the central North Island ranges.

On a steep ridge 1500 metres above sea level, Brian Pickering had been caught out. Though he was a hugely experienced tramper and search-and-rescue volunteer with a formidable knowledge of the bush, he'd never known conditions like it. The air temperature had dropped below zero and snow was falling, but the real potential killer was the 130 kilometre per hour icy winds that were lowering the wind chill factor to minus 30 degrees Celsius.

Still, if anyone could survive it, the expertly equipped Rotorua man could. He was ten kilometres into the first day of a week-long 86-kilometre solo tramp, and he knew it was too late to back out. He'd passed the halfway mark for the day's walk and his best chance was to fight on to the next hut, about an hour away. He just needed to get across the windswept ridge, where the only shelter was rock and tussock, and leg it down to the hut.

The big Yorkshire-born man knew there were two trampers ahead of him—he had seen their tracks in the snow—but he was stunned shortly before 5 p.m. to round a bend and encounter their shivering figures huddled on the ground. Pickering guessed immediately they were suffering from hypothermia. One didn't even have the strength to undo the straps on his pack. In the words of a search and rescue expert who later became involved, 'They had sat down to die.'

'They were in a mess,' Pickering later told a reporter. 'I didn't even have to talk to them to know they were not in a good way.'

They were John and Matthew Painting, an Auckland man and his 13-year-old son. They too had set out that day, for a four-day camp, but had stopped for a rest half an hour earlier and hadn't had the strength to get up again. Though they were wearing Swanndris, their cotton under-layers were soaked and were dragging their body temperatures down. They were equipped for a few nights in the bush, but not for alpine conditions.

The pair were in no state to move, so Pickering figured they were going to have to bunker down as best they could. Though the trio had two tents between them, neither had been made to withstand such fearsome conditions. Pickering figured he'd better try to erect one anyway, but in the buffeting winds he found it impossible.

Instead he pulled the pair into a shallow hollow, stuffed them into their sleeping bags and wrapped them up in the tents and whatever other gear he could find. He also forced them to eat. Then he got out his mobile phone. They were in luck—he had a signal. Had they been just a little further on, they would have been out of contact with the world. He rang 111 and shortly afterwards search and rescue co-ordinator Senior Constable Cliff Jones of the Turangi Police got word of the trio's predicament.

Pickering could then, of course, have left the Paintings in the hope the rescuers would find them and continued on to the hut to save himself. The thought didn't occur to him. He chose to share their fate, though an icy darkness was beginning to fall.

With his own body temperature dropping quickly despite his many layers of good-quality bushwear, Pickering dished out a constant supply of high-energy food and kept the father and son talking—about work, school, hunting, anything to keep them alert and prevent them falling into a dangerous sleep. The winds were howling so much he had to shout, even though the pair were centimetres away. After a few hours the father and son could do little but grunt in reply.

Meanwhile, back in Turangi, Jones was scrambling a search team. Someone even unwittingly rang Pickering's home to ask him to help, figuring his expertise would be invaluable. His was always one of the first phone numbers on the list when such assistance was needed.

That evening a team of searchers left Turangi, with the storm roaring in their ears. Even in the town, tornadoes had ripped up buildings and trees. The team of men, Terry Blumhardt, Brendan Dobbyn and Kevin Singer, drove as far into the bush as they could, then set out on foot. It was a five-kilometre climb to the ridge line, then they would have to battle along the track across the tops for another five and a half kilometres, in pitch darkness with the storm still screaming around them.

After a few hours they realised how hopeless the task was. It was taking them two and a half hours to cover a single kilometre. At times the blizzard forced them onto their hands and knees. To stand up was to risk being picked up by the wind and flung off a cliff. At one point Dobbyn, who weighed 100 kilograms and was carrying a heavy pack, was spun around like a top by the wind. They persisted as long as they could but, at 3.30 a.m., with their own lives in danger, they reluctantly heeded an order to turn back.

'You could hear the wind howling in the background during their radio broadcasts,' Jones said later.

Jones had the tough job of calling Pickering to let him know. He could hear the desperation in the Rotorua man's voice. His strength had audibly faded during the night.

'We sat here in absolute despair as we listened to it unfold,' Jones later told a reporter. 'We were speaking to him on the hour and it was getting worse and worse. Their conditions were deteriorating and deteriorating.'

Pickering had by then bundled the Paintings into the same sleeping bag so they could conserve what little heat remained in their bodies. His body too was beginning to shut down.

Shortly before 4 a.m. the regular phone communication between the base and the trio suddenly stopped. With no answer to his calls, Jones didn't know whether the trampers were dead or alive.

A second rescue team was hurriedly assembled. It took Shaun Campbell, Hugo Verhagen and Kerry Palmer three hours to get to the tree line. They reached the top of the ridge as a dreary dawn broke. At one point Verhagen was blown into a crevasse and had to be extracted by his fellow searchers. In places they had to trudge through knee-deep snow drifts. The gusts were so strong they had trouble breathing and had to huddle together at times to avoid being blown over.

'You are talking wind that if you put your head up it would snap you backwards,' recalled Jones. 'It was driving heavy ice and snow.'

After they'd been battling the ridgeline for three hours the searchers began to doubt they were going to make it to the trio. They were forced to make a call on whether to turn back. They all agreed—they would continue.

'We didn't fear so much for ourselves,' said Verhagen later. 'We feared for the people that were up there, knowing they were suffering in those conditions—they were horrific.'

The stranded trampers had by then been hunkered down for more than twelve hours. Then, at 9.15 a.m., Jones' phone rang again. It was Pickering. His mobile phone battery had died and he was so cold that it had taken him until then—more than five hours later—to summon up the strength to crawl five metres to a pack and retrieve another phone.

Jones could sense that Pickering guessed how close he was getting to death. 'He had to know that when we were speaking to him . . . I could hear it in his voice. We said to him, "Are you going to help us here . . . come through for us," and he said, "I'll do my best." It was gut-wrenching stuff.'

It was late morning by the time the four searchers got to the trio—about 17 hours after Pickering had come across the Paintings. They were alive but suffering from severe hypothermia. John Painting was worst affected. It was going to be impossible for the search team to get them out on foot. They had no choice but to put the trio through at least another night in the bush, until the weather cleared long enough to get a rescue helicopter to retrieve them.

At least the search team had brought plenty of supplies. Within five minutes of arriving they'd put dry clothes on the Paintings and erected a tent designed for the conditions. Pickering later remembered seeing a thermometer on one of the rescuer's packs. When he'd arrived it had read minus four. Once the trio were snuggled into the tent, it was at 17 degrees. 'Almost like summer,' he said later.

After three hours another search team arrived at the spot and put up three more tents. Pickering had an afternoon snack of noodles and sweet milky tea, then gratefully went to sleep. The wind was beginning to subside and Campbell, Verhagen and Palmer retreated on foot back to base.

The following day a window opened in the storm and Kevin Singer—a member of the first search team—finally made it to the trampers, this time as part of a rescue helicopter crew. Pickering and the Paintings were flown to safety.

Pickering had by then rallied to the point that his only health concern was a sore throat—a symptom of his efforts to keep the Paintings alert and talking. 'I had to yell at the top of my voice . . . You couldn't hear anything above the howling wind. When we got back to Turangi the first thing I did was stop at a dairy and get some Throaties because my throat was so sore.'

When Jones caught up with the Paintings again six weeks later, they still had no feeling in their hands and feet. It was evident they would have died without Pickering's help and the bravery of the rescue teams who'd tracked them down.

'Thank God he was there,' said John Painting of Pickering. 'We owe that guy so much . . . we were lucky to come out at all.'

Jones lost no time nominating Pickering for a bravery award. In 2005 he received the New Zealand Bravery Decoration, one of the country's highest bravery honours. 'He knew when he made the decision to stay with them that it could cost him his life,' said Jones. 'He saved their lives and he's a hero.'

The men in the first two rescue teams—Blumhardt, Dobbyn, Singer, Palmer, Verhagen and Campbell—received the New Zealand Bravery Medal, the next decoration down in the official award hierarchy.

Pickering told a reporter he believed the men in the rescue teams were, in many ways, braver than he was. 'What they did was more than I did, because I came across it and could not do something about it. But they actually volunteered to come out.'

He said he didn't consider himself a hero. 'I was just the right person in the right place at the right time. I could have chosen to do my tramp the day before and nobody would have found them. It was pure coincidence.'

George

Warrior terrier

Just before noon on 29 April 2007, eleven-year-old Richard Rosewarne and his four younger siblings set out for a walk around their neighbourhood. The small south Taranaki town of Manaia was always quiet on a Sunday.

Richard pushed three-year-old Ariana Wilson in her stroller, while four-year-old Darryl Wilson skipped alongside. Kelly, ten, and Christian Rosewarne, eight, followed close behind, enjoying the autumn sunshine.

Out in front ran George, an elderly Jack Russell terrier and firm friend of the children. George belonged to their next-door neighbour, 69-year-old Alan Gay. He was a quiet, humble little dog who often sat under the letterbox for hours waiting patiently for his beloved owner to come home. George was fourteen years old and had a serious heart condition, but he loved to play rugby with the children in the front yard and often accompanied them on neighbourhood jaunts.

George and the children had just turned a corner when they heard a menacing growl behind them. Richard looked over his shoulder. Two pit bull terriers were charging across the grass verge, rapidly closing in on his youngest brother.

'There's a dog!' he shouted, grabbing Darryl's hand. 'Run!'

The children began to run, screaming and crying, but in his panic Darryl let go of Richard's hand. The older boy had to stop to let his little brother go ahead. The dogs were almost upon them.

Then George stopped too. He turned around and began barking. He ran straight into the path of the snarling dogs. The little dog bravely stood his ground as the pit bulls closed in.

The children kept running until they reached the corner of the block. Tears were streaming down their faces. There they turned. They stood, horrified, as the two pit bulls savagely attacked George, ripping the skin from his throat, chest and back. He tried to shake them off, but the tiny old terrier was no match for the larger dogs' brute strength. There was nothing the children could do to help him.

'George tried to protect us by barking and rushing at them, but they started to bite him—one on the head and the other on the back,' Richard Rosewarne later told a journalist. 'We ran off crying and some people saw what was happening and rescued George.'

George was rushed to Hawera, but it was too late to save him. The vet, Steven Hopkinson, told the *Taranaki Daily News* that George's injuries were the worst he'd seen. Even if he'd made it through surgery, there would have been no guarantee he would live.

Alan Gay made the heart-wrenching decision to have his loyal companion put down. 'George was brave—he took them on, and he's not even a foot high,' Gay told the Associated Press. 'He jumped in on them, he tried to keep them off. If it wasn't for George, those kids would have copped it.'

The two pit bulls were picked up by dog control authorities at their Manaia home and destroyed.

George's bravery made headlines around the world and tributes flowed from Canada, the United States, Sweden and Australia. In Austin, Texas, 58-year-old former marine Jerrell Hudman was so moved by George's sacrifice that he sent Gay one of three Purple Heart medals awarded when he was wounded in combat in Vietnam in 1967, in memory of the 'little warrior'.

One week after George's death, the SPCA awarded George the Supreme Award for Bravery, a medal usually given to humans who demonstrate bravery in aiding animals. George was the first recipient of the award since 1990.

'It was an extraordinary act of heroism,' chief executive Robyn Kippenberger said. 'It says a huge amount for the animal-human bond that he actually went in to save them. That he weighed into a couple of dogs considerably larger than himself, clearly to protect a child, is just a most amazing act and needs to be recognised.'

For months the accolades continued to flow. In October a bronze statue of a jaunty, wagging George was unveiled on a rock in the Manaia town centre. A Swedish pop group, the Talkabouts, even wrote a song inspired by George's courageous exploits.

On 12 February 2009, a tearful Alan Gay stood before a small crowd at Manaia's band rotunda as Governor-General Anand Satyanand presented him with Britain's PDSA Gold Medal. The medal is considered the animal equivalent of the George Cross, the United Kingdom's highest civilian award for bravery. The five children George protected that day—Richard, Kelly, Christian, Darryl and Ariana—stood by Gay's side.

Presenting the award, Satyanand described George as 'the perfect example of a hero dog'. He said that George exemplified the best attributes of the Jack Russell breed, often said to be a 'big dog in a little dog's body'.

The mayor of South Taranaki, Ross Dunlop, read the citation from PDSA director general Jan McLoughlin. 'There's no doubt that George was a small dog with a lion's share of courage. Each account of his devotion to the five children that day tells of a dog that was not afraid to face great fear in order to protect his friends. The children will never forget George's sacrifice and PDSA is proud to honour this exceptionally brave dog.'

George was only the 15th recipient of the medal. Upon learning of the award, Gay had told the *Taranaki Daily News*, 'I feel good about receiving it, but I hope it's the last one because George is dead and all this has gone on long enough.'

After the ceremony, Gay and the Rosewarne and Wilson children crossed the street to the little bronze statue. In a final act of honour, they placed the royal-blue ribbon of the PDSA medal around George's neck.

Tony McClean

The teacher who wouldn't leave a student behind

Auckland teacher Tony McClean might not have known just how close he was to death when he leapt into the swollen Mangatepopo Gorge on 15 April 2008. But he must have known that strapping a disabled student to himself wasn't going to improve his chances of survival.

Early that afternoon the popular 29-year-old had set out to go canyoning in the central North Island gorge with ten of his students from Elim Christian College in Howick, Auckland. They were led there along a bush track by Jodie Sullivan, an instructor from the Sir Edmund Hillary Outdoor Pursuits Centre.

It had been raining for about 24 hours and, as student Kish Proctor later recalled, the track was so wet it was like walking down a waterfall. 'It was heavy, heavy rain. It wasn't like normal, it wasn't easing up. It was heavy rain.'

About 1 p.m. the group reached their starting point, a spot below a hydro power dam. As the excited students played games, Sullivan checked the water in the steep, narrow gorge, which was prone to flash flooding. Rain was falling and the river had risen slightly but the water was clear and she could still see rocks protruding from the current above the dam so she was confident it wasn't engorged.

She led the group into the water, planning to be out of the gorge by 3 p.m.

What Sullivan didn't know was that the MetService had upgraded its earlier prediction of rain to a thunderstorm warning. The update never made it to the Outdoor Pursuits Centre. In fact, rainwater was beginning to cascade down Mt Tongariro, rapidly swelling creeks and streams, hundreds of which drained straight into the gorge. The weather that afternoon was later described as a 'rain bomb'.

By the time the group reached its halfway mark—where there was an alternative exit route—there was no sign of the approaching danger. But it was getting dark as the storm set in. Student Ashley Smith, who wasn't wearing her usual prescription glasses, was finding it hard to see and was relying on her hands and feet to guide her along. She was getting scared.

Although they had planned to make it to a plunge pool further along, Sullivan recognised that some of the students were afraid, so turned them around to head back downstream to the dam. As they crossed the river, she noticed the water had become murky and was beginning to rise.

By the time the group neared the valley's deepest point, the water was coming up rapidly and the current was picking up speed. Crossing the river became difficult and Sullivan started to use a throwbag—a bag attached to a rope that she would toss into the water so the students could catch it and be pulled or swept safely to the bank. Eventually it just became too difficult. They climbed to a ledge above the roaring water. They were just 135 metres from their intended exit point.

Sullivan and the young teacher, Tony McClean, searched for a safe way out. But the ledge was sheltered by an overhang so they couldn't climb out. They couldn't go upstream. And a blind corner lay downstream, beyond which was the 7-metre dam, which emptied out onto huge rocks and fallen logs.

They figured their best chance was to wait it out and hope the river level would drop.

It didn't. At 2.30 p.m. it had been running at 4.6 cubic metres per second. Within 90 minutes it had reached 17 cubic metres per second—equivalent to the normal flow of the much wider Tongariro River.

The charismatic McClean knew he had to keep the students calm. He led them in silly songs, told them to be strong and brave and tempted them with promises of hot showers back at camp.

But it soon became apparent that the water level wasn't subsiding. As they sat on the ledge it rose until it was surging around their ankles, then their knees. Eventually they were forced to stand and hold on to the rock face to prevent being swept downstream. Sullivan positioned herself at the bottom edge of the ledge to catch anyone who lost their footing. McClean was at the upstream end, battling an increasingly strong current. It seemed obvious that if they waited any longer they would be swept away.

Sullivan tried to call for help with her radio but there was no signal. She came up with a new plan: they would jump into the water at five minute intervals, singly or in pairs, round the blind corner and swim fast for the bank before the torrent swept them over the dam. She would go first and then use a throwbag and rope to help the others to the bank. The river was so thunderous that she had to shout her instructions. Even then McClean had to repeat them to several of his students.

Before each student jumped, McClean prayed with them. Student Ashley Smith was to be the first to enter the water, attached to Sullivan with a carabiner. She was terrified.

She later wrote: 'I was freaking out but [McClean] held me and said, "Don't worry, Ash, you can do this. I know you can because I will be praying for you." And right then everyone gathered around me, hugged me and prayed.'

So Sullivan and Smith hit the churning water. Though they were battered by the current they made it around the corner and reached the bank just before the dam, as planned. Kish Proctor volunteered to go next. But as he rounded the corner it was immediately obvious there was no way he was going to make it to Sullivan or her rope—he was a good seven metres away and was being pulled under the water. He was swept past her and down the dam, hitting a log and rocks, but managed to scramble ashore. He looked at his watch. It was 4 p.m. In ones and twos the others followed. Just one—Peter Shih—managed to grab the throwbag and was hauled ashore. The others either couldn't catch the bag or couldn't hold onto it in the maelstrom.

Smith later recalled the moment that Floyd Fernandes and Anthony Mulder rounded the bend, attached to each other: 'Jodie threw the rope but—I don't know what happened—but it didn't reach them. They were too far on the other side. And then I was standing there and then Floyd and Anthony looked at me and Floyd started calling out for help . . . and Anthony lifted up his hand for me to grab but I couldn't reach it. I watched as they were thrown over the dam.'

Soon two people were left on the ledge—McClean and 16-year-old Taiwanese student Tom Hsu, who had cerebral palsy. And still the river rose.

McClean couldn't see what was going on downstream, and couldn't hear anything above the roar of the water. He didn't know that just two of the nine students who had already gone into the water had made it to the bank above the dam—Smith and Shih. The others had all been swept over the dam—five to their deaths.

Still, he was fit and a strong swimmer. Alone he would have had a good chance of survival. But there was no way he was going alone.

Though Hsu, by all accounts, was always determined not to let his disability slow him down, it was clear that the conditions that day were perilous for even the most able-bodied of teenagers. And though Hsu's legs were relatively strong, his hands were severely affected by the condition and he was not confident in the water. To complicate matters, he had left his prescription glasses at the camp.

So McClean made what to him was the natural decision—he hooked Hsu to him and leapt into the churning water. It was the best way to increase Hsu's chances, even if it cut his own.

No living person can say exactly what happened next. But the battered bodies of the teacher and his student were the last to be found, still joined together, about three kilometres downstream of the dam.

Of the twelve people who had set out on the canyoning trip that day, only five survived: Sullivan, Proctor, Smith, Shih and Sarah Brooks. Seven died: McClean, Hsu, Mulder, Fernandes, Natasha Bray, Portia McPhail and Tara Gregory. All the students were aged just 16.

Coroner Chris Devonport later said the courage of all those in the group could not be underestimated. He added: 'Mr McClean appears to have assisted Ms Sullivan and the students in whatever way he was able, and tragically lost his life assisting a less able student down the stream.'

As the story of McClean's sacrifice emerged, those close to him were not surprised.

'When the police lady told me that I thought, "That's him,"' his father, John McClean, told a reporter. 'I was proud of him. I looked at [his body] and I knew he had struggled—he would have struggled for those kids, struggled for his own life.'

His mother, Jeanette McClean, who worked at the same school as her son and knew Hsu well, was grateful her son hadn't been alone. 'He had Tom's loving arms wrapped around him.'

She was 'enormously proud' that in the most traumatic moment of his life—and in fact the last moment of his life—he stayed true to his strong values.

‘We were thankful that Tony had not died alone as they both struggled against the force of nature, and this time, sadly, nature won.’

She recalled a speech he’d made in 2006 that had become almost prophetic: ‘He talked about how, as a Christian . . . you could even be called to give up your life.’

McClean’s girlfriend, Ruth Nixon, told a reporter: ‘Those kids on that ledge, although that was the last half-hour of their lives, they were happy, they felt safe. He made them feel secure.’

His friend Jonno Ward said, ‘I’m so proud he gave his life trying to save others; leading, encouraging, praying and struggling for a person who couldn’t save himself.’

In an editorial, the *New Zealand Herald* said McClean’s ‘bravery and instinctive behaviour in doing what was right struck an especially deep chord in a society that is said often to be increasingly individualistic and uncaring of one another.’

‘The impact was profound. Throughout New Zealand, people paused and wondered whether they would have had the fortitude to act as . . . Mr McClean did.’

2.
WARRIORS

Hone Heke

Flagpole warrior

Hone Heke's famous first assault on the flagpole at Kororareka has gone down in history as one of the most infamous acts of the 19th century. But it was no random act of mindless vandalism. Nor was it supposed to be an act of war.

In fact, he'd put it there in the first place. Heke had donated the pole some years earlier to fly a Maori flag but it had been commandeered by the English for their own colours. To Heke, the Union flag came to symbolise the depredation and despair brought by the colonists.

Heke had good reason to be disappointed in the treatment of his Ngapuhi people by the British settlers. Born Heke Pokai, he had spent some of his teenage years studying at the Kerikeri mission school under Henry Williams and in his late twenties he was baptised and changed his name to Hone, a Maori transliteration of John. He had taken on the English religion and an English name, but he would never turn his back on his people.

Though British missionaries were well established in the North by the 1830s, the British government was keen to enshrine a formal agreement under which it could claim the country as a colony. In early 1840 Governor William Hobson had the Treaty of Waitangi drafted in both English and Maori and presented it to a group of gathered chiefs at Waitangi. Among their number was Hone Heke.

There was much discussion. Heke is quoted as saying to Hobson,

'Governor, you should stay with us and be like a father. If you go away, then the French and the rum sellers will take us Maori over.'

Heke firmly believed the colonists would remain true to their word to protect the rights of Maori if the chiefs proclaimed their allegiance to the British Crown. His trust was so complete that he was among the first to sign the treaty. He saw it as a way of protecting the rights of his people. He did not think for a second that he was signing those rights away.

It wasn't long before the chief started to lose faith in the promises made in the treaty. In 1841 the colony's capital was transferred from Kororareka to Auckland, causing economic hardship in the North. The number of ships visiting the town fell, demand for land in the area dropped and those Maori who had worked for and with the colonists found themselves out of work. Alongside this economic depression came the enforcement of British law in the region. Maori were not happy to find themselves being expected to kowtow to the Crown, when they had been prepared to work alongside it as equals.

As he watched his people sink further into despair, Heke felt taunted by the Union flag flying above Kororareka. So, early on the morning of 8 July 1844, he led his men up to the flagstaff and cut it down. He had intended that the act would send a political message to the government, but the local settlers took fright. Chaos erupted in the town. Governor Robert FitzRoy called on the colony of New South Wales to send military help, though calm was restored before they arrived. Heke wrote to FitzRoy to offer peace:

Friend Governor,
This is my speech to you. My disobedience and rudeness is no new thing. I inherit it from my parents, from my ancestors, do not imagine it is a new feature in my character, but I am thinking of leaving off my rude conduct to Europeans. Now I say that I will prepare

another pole inland at Waimate, and I will erect it at its proper place at Kororareka, in order to put a stop to our present quarrel. Let your soldiers remain beyond sea and at Auckland, do not send them here. The pole that was cut down belonged to me, I made it for the native Flag, and it was never paid for by the Europeans.

From your friend,
Hone Heke Pokai
Waimate, July 19 1844

Despite Heke's promise to behave, he had no intention of backing down in the fight for the rights of his people. True to his word, he replaced the flagpole at Kororareka. And then he took it down again.

With no obvious improvement to the treatment of Maori, Heke felled his new pole on 10 January 1845. A furious FitzRoy put a bounty of £100 on the chief's head. No one took him up on the offer, and Heke even managed to hack down a third flagpole on 19 January. He was determined to make his point: that the colonial government should be held to the commitments they made at Waitangi.

The government was equally determined to subdue what they saw as a brewing rebellion in the north. FitzRoy ordered a new flagpole and despatched a battalion to the town to protect it.

Heke saw this as a hostile act. On 11 March, he and fellow chief Kawiti led 1100 Maori warriors into Kororareka. After creating a diversion to distract the troops, his men managed to drop the pole for the fourth and final time. The flagpole had become a joke. An increasingly frustrated George Grey—newly appointed governor—took exception and fierce fighting broke out. The British naval ship *Hazard* even began bombarding the entire settlement. Both British and Maori troops sacked the town, though Heke ordered his men to leave the Anglican church and the Catholic bishop's house untouched.

Heke then moved inland to a pa near Lake Omapere before building a fortified settlement at Okaihau. This new pa was attacked by a colonial force on 8 May 1845 but the fortifications were so strong that the invaders were unable to make any headway. Heke, true to his Christian beliefs, ensured that the British dead received a Christian burial.

Heke continued to fight until he received a severe thigh wound in a skirmish. While he was recuperating, he penned a letter to Grey. It said, 'God made this country for us. It cannot be sliced; if it were a whale it might be sliced. Return to your own country, which was made by God for you. God made this land for us; it is not for any stranger or foreign nation to meddle with this sacred country.'

Between his famous fight with the flagpole, and his gentlemanly conduct even when fighting colonial troops, Heke became something of a folk hero. It helped that he took pains to avoid causing any hardship for European settlers. Heke considered that his fight was against the colonial government, which he considered had broken the promises it made under the Treaty of Waitangi. He did not want the Europeans to leave his land, he merely wanted them to keep their word.

Historian James Cowan wrote in 1935: 'Heke's war was waged in a knightly fashion strange to remember in these unchivalrous days. When the troops marched inland against him in 1845, he regarded them in a semi-friendly way, not at all the manner of a professional soldier. He laid no ambuscades; he cut no communications; he waylaid no supply convoys. Some of his young men even took pity on the soldiers and gave them assistance in the bush. He did not interfere with non-combatants; in fact, he made the war something like a chivalrous tournament. The heavily-equipped soldiers were helpless in the bush; they could all have been cut off and destroyed had the Maoris been so inclined. There was no fighting at night. Civilised nations have changed all that!'

Heke made peace with Grey in 1848. In the end, the man who fought hard against colonial rule was taken down by a colonial disease: tuberculosis. He died in Kaikohe in 1850. He was thought to have been in his early forties.

'Heke is the popular hero of the North,' wrote Cowan. 'He was the hero of most of the Maori tribes when the news of the war went forth. Mention of Heke still brings tears of affection to many Ngapuhi eyes.'

William Malone

Hero of Gallipoli

Quinn's Post
5/8/15 [about 10pm]
'Dear old England. She is in a muddle right enough, but comes out all right in the end. And there is no country like her. If only we can knock a bit more thoroughness into her, as a matter of course it would help wonderfully. My candle is all burnt out and we will soon be moving. So good night, dearest one. With all my love.'

These were the last words that Lieutenant Colonel William George Malone wrote to his beloved wife, Ida, before he led his Wellington Battalion on what would become one of New Zealand's most famous military stands—the assault on Chunuk Bair.

Malone was a transplanted Englishman, who had emigrated to New Zealand at the age of 21, and he had good cause to think his former countrymen to be 'in a muddle'. On 25 April 1915 he and his battalion were among thousands of soldiers who were landed on the Gallipoli Peninsula as the British attempted to gain control of the strategic Dardanelles waterway. In his diary that day Malone described soldiers 'being sent to chaos and slaughter, nay murder'.

At the age of 56, Malone was easily the oldest man in the Wellington Battalion but his age proved to be no barrier when it came to leading from the front. He was physically strong and fit and he expected only the best from himself and his men. An acquaintance described the soldier as 'a typical old New Zealand pioneer with a powerful jaw and an appearance of great strength and determination'.

Prior to landing in Turkey, the New Zealanders had trained in Egypt. While there, Malone had set about ensuring that his battalion were well prepared for combat. He drove his men hard. Though some resented him for it at the time, once they were in the heat of battle the lessons he had taught saved numerous lives.

Malone's military knowledge came from a mixture of service—as a commander of the Armed Constabulary in Taranaki—and an avid study of military history. This combination of practical experience and military knowledge was to stand him in good stead in the chaos that was Gallipoli. He knew that it was important to provide strong leadership and practical help to men who were frightened and disheartened at having seen so many of their comrades killed and wounded.

Malone did not shy away from standing up for his men. When, on 13 May, an English battery's shelling caused shrapnel and pieces of shell to rain down on the Wellington Battalion's quarters, he 'went down and told them they were very rude and that if they shot us up any more we should have to shoot back!' This was typical of Malone's directness and willingness to take on anyone who put his men at unnecessary risk.

Malone's dogged support of his men didn't win him many fans among his superiors in Turkey and, as time wore on, the feeling became increasingly mutual. One officer with whom he clashed was his New Zealand Infantry Brigade commander, Brigadier General Francis Johnston. In early August, just days before the assault on Chunuk Bair, Malone wrote in his diary, 'The Brigadier will not get down to bed rock. He seems to think a night attack is like "kissing one's hand" . . . He is an extraordinary man. If it were not so serious it would be laughable. So far as I am concerned the men, my brave gallant men, shall have the best fighting chance I can give them or that can be got. No airy plunging and disregard of the rules and chances.'

Chunuk Bair was a key strategic summit on the range overlooking the bay now called Anzac Cove. The assault on it was, in part, intended to break a stalemate between the Allied troops and their Turkish counterparts. By capturing the summit, the commander in charge of the Gallipoli campaign, General Sir Ian Hamilton, planned to clear the slopes of Turkish defenders and secure the whole area.

While other Allied troops undertook diversionary attacks at Lone Pine and Helles, the Kiwi troops set out for Chunuk Bair. The Wellington Battalion, as part of the New Zealand Infantry Brigade, were to undertake a key role in the offensive by securing the Apex on Rhodendron Ridge, about 500 metres below Chunuk Bair.

They were supposed to meet another group of soldiers at the Apex and together push on to capture Chunuk Bair. The other soldiers, for various reasons, failed to arrive but the Allied commanders insisted that the attack continue. Mid-morning on 7 August, the Auckland Battalion had managed to get within 200 metres of the summit but the casualties sustained by the battalion were massive and the ridge remained in Turkish hands.

The command went out for the Wellington Battalion to continue the attack. Malone could see that sending his men out into Turkish fire in the middle of the day was futile. He flatly refused orders that would effectively mean sacrificing his men for little gain. Johnston eventually agreed that the attack should take place at night.

Early the following morning, 8 August, Malone led the men of the Wellington Battalion towards the summit of Chunuk Bair. The attack surprised the Turks and they abandoned their position. But it wasn't long before they were firing on the New Zealanders holding Chunuk Bair. Malone and his men had little choice but to return fire while waiting for reinforcements.

The fighting continued with a fury. At 5 p.m., Allied shells meant for the Turks exploded over Malone's trench. Shrapnel rained down and killed the nuggety Kiwi commander.

When reinforcements finally arrived, they found only 70 of the Wellington Battalion's 760 men still standing. Malone's earlier refusal to sacrifice his men turned out, ultimately, to be futile. But it's fitting that even in his last days he was still putting his men's interests first.

Despite the huge human losses sustained during the campaign and the fact that the vantage point was only held for two days, the seizure of Chunuk Bair is still thought to be one of the few successes of the Gallipoli campaign and this was largely down to the expertise of William Malone.

Malone's body was never recovered. A plaque commemorating his life lies in the Grand Hall at Parliament and his statue stands in his Taranaki hometown of Stratford.

Leslie Averill

Liberator

'Doc Averill is one of the promising young men in the city's medical forces who is rapidly making himself felt in the community as a clever diagnostician and a man with a wizard touch in surgery.'

So said *New Zealand Truth* of Christchurch doctor Leslie Averill in January 1928. But it wasn't the first time that the man's name had featured in the pages of that august publication, and in previous years they hadn't been nearly as supportive.

In 1916, nineteen-year-old Averill was studying medicine at Auckland University when he and a friend decided to volunteer for active service in World War I. He did his basic training at Trentham Military Camp in Wellington, then earned a commission to become an officer in the 34th Reinforcements of the New Zealand Expeditionary Force.

It was this commission that first earned him the attention of *New Zealand Truth*. It published an article claiming that, far from earning his commission, Averill had been given it because his father, Walter, was the Anglican Bishop of Auckland.

In fact, Averill's parents had reservations about him joining the army, and he'd passed the officer's exam with flying colours. His actions over the coming years would prove that the Army's faith in this young officer was well placed.

Despite signing up in 1916, Averill didn't leave New Zealand until February 1918. On arrival in England, he joined the New

Zealand Rifle Brigade at Brocton Camp in Staffordshire as second lieutenant. By May the brigade had been posted to fight on the Western Front in France. In August 1918 Averill was awarded a Military Cross for gallantry and leadership for his actions in the assault on Bapaume, a fortified town in northern France.

But it was another fortified town, just 65 kilometres away, where Lieutenant Leslie Averill would make his name as a Kiwi hero. On 4 November 1918, the New Zealand Division made huge gains on the Western Front. They managed to advance ten kilometres, capturing more than 2000 German soldiers along the way. As they swept eastwards, the plan was to bypass the strongly fortified town of Le Quesnoy.

Nearly 2000 German soldiers had been holed up there since 1914 and the town's 1500 residents were at the mercy of the invaders. Le Quesnoy's ramparts were originally built in 1536 but had been added to many times since. With two sets of high walls and a moat running around the town it was a key strategic point for German troops. In order to capture the town, Allied military leaders figured they would have to shell it heavily. To do that would mean massive loss of civilian life.

The New Zealand Rifle Brigade, under the command of Major Harold Barrowclough, thought they'd give it a crack anyway. The troops surrounded the town and engaged in a gun battle with the German garrison. A German prisoner-of-war was sent into town at about 10 a.m. to tell his countrymen that surrender was the only option. Clearly they didn't agree.

With bombardment out of the question because of the French people sheltering inside, the Kiwis decided to take a simple approach to liberating the town. They got a ladder.

By midday, Averill and some of the men from his platoon had scaled the outer walls of the town and searched for a way to breach the town's inner wall.

Averill describes what they found:

> 'The 30-foot ladder was too short to reach from the bottom of the moat to the top of the final wall but there was one place where the ladder could be placed to reach the top. This was on a narrow stone bridge, about a foot wide, which spanned the moat and was connected with a sluice-gate . . . After crossing this bridge and sluice-gate a narrow ledge ran for some 10 yards beside the wall to an arched opening, giving entrance to the town . . . It was only on this narrow wall above the sluice-gate that the ladder could reach the top.'

He returned to headquarters and reported to Barrowclough that he'd managed to find a way into the town. The major agreed that it was worth a try and Averill and his men returned to make an attempt on the inner wall. While they made their move on the ramparts, their countrymen let loose with a barrage of covering fire that sent the German guards running from their posts.

Once Averill and his men reached the narrow wall above the sluice gate, they laid their ladder against it. Two men held the ladder steady while Averill climbed onto the ramparts. A German sentry spotted him and ran off to warn his colleagues. Averill, followed by several gunners, gave chase and captured the German platoon.

New Zealand soldiers swarmed onto and over the walls, while at the other end of town more of their countrymen managed to breach the Valenciennes gate. The Germans fought valiantly but soon realised they had little choice but to surrender.

The townspeople of Le Quesnoy were delighted to be freed from four years of German occupation and they took to the streets, greeting the New Zealanders with flowers, cakes and kisses. One New Zealand officer found it all a little too much, later remarking they 'freely embraced them in a manner peculiar to the French but most embarrassing to the stoic New Zealanders'.

Although the town survived the day with little damage, 43 members of the Rifle Brigade lost their lives and some 250 were injured. Their deaths were made all the more poignant by the fact that the Armistice was signed just a week later and theirs were some of the last lives lost in the war.

The town of Le Quesnoy has never forgotten the exploits of Averill and his compatriots on 4 November 1914. It remains the focus of Anzac Day commemorations for New Zealanders and locals alike and Kiwis are welcomed there with open arms.

Averill was appointed a Citoyen d'Honneur (Citizen of Honour) of the town in 1968 and in 1973 he was appointed a Chevalier de le Legion d'Honneur—the highest award given by France for outstanding service to that country. There is also a street and a school in Le Quesnoy named after Averill.

Just a few metres from where Averill breached the wall now stands a memorial depicting the exploits of the Rifle Brigade with the words, 'In honour of the men of New Zealand through whose valour the town of Le Quesnoy was restored to France.'

Eric Griffiths
Doug Jolly
Geoffrey Cox

Civil warriors

'I'm afraid you're for it, Geoffrey. We've still no word of what has happened to Denis so you are to go to Madrid straight away.'

With those words from Geoffrey Cox's editor at London's *News Chronicle*, the Palmerston North-born, Invercargill-raised newsman was despatched to Spain as a war correspondent. It would be no junket—his predecessor, Denis Weaver, had been captured by dictator Francisco Franco's troops on account of the paper's pro-Republican stance and was still missing.

The 26-year-old had arrived in Europe on a Rhodes Scholarship to Oxford in 1932. Like most young antipodean travellers, Cox had spent some time travelling in Europe. In 1934, while visiting an Oxford colleague in Germany, he was invited to attend a Nazi rally in Nuremberg led by a man called Adolf Hitler. It gave him an unsettling early insight into the threat of fascism in Europe.

In 1935, Cox had joined the *News Chronicle* as a junior reporter. He was seen as a relatively expendable writer to send into the chaos of the Spanish Civil War.

He arrived in Spain on 28 October 1936 with some reservations. 'The sunshine, the blue skies and blue sea, the long empty coastline and the dusty brown plains reminded me of New Zealand,' he wrote later. 'What was I doing, waiting to go to war, so far from home?'

Madrid was then under siege on three sides from Franco's troops. The Republican stronghold was a coveted prize. Just before midnight on 28 October, Cox filed his first story from the blacked-out city. It made the front page of the next morning's *Daily Chronicle*. And so began his dogged mission to keep the British public informed of the fascist wave that was taking hold of Europe.

In his book *Eyewitness*, Cox tells of an encounter with another Kiwi later that evening. 'Half an hour later—even in wartime, Madrid dined late—I found myself eating a huge Spanish omelette and drinking Rioja in a small Basque restaurant with [Jan] Yindrich [a Spanish journalist] and a New Zealander from Wellington with his arm in a sling, who had been wounded in the shoulder when flying a fighter plane for the Republic.'

That pilot was Eric Griffiths, the only New Zealander to fly in the Republican Air Force's international squadron. It was formed after the majority of the pilots in the Spanish air force sided with Franco. Griffiths routinely put his life on the line flying sorties for the Republican cause.

When the civil war had broken out in mid-1936, the 24-year-old was based in England. He immediately volunteered to ferry aircraft from the United Kingdom to Republican Spain. On one of these delivery sortees he was asked to become a fighter pilot for the Republicans.

It was a tempting offer, and not just for altruistic reasons—his contract promised him £200 for each enemy aircraft he managed to shoot down and £1000 in the event that he was badly injured. The Wellingtonian signed up and was promptly posted to the Getafe airfield near Madrid.

It was dangerous work. His squadron sent up ten-year-old aircraft against modern and fast German and Italian aeroplanes.

In the nine months that Griffiths served, 16 of his squadron's 20 pilots were killed. He still managed to take out four enemy aircraft and was paid the promised £200 for each of them.

Even though he was quickly gaining experience, it was only a matter of time before Griffiths was injured. He and another pilot were on patrol over Toledo in September 1936 when they came under attack. A bullet exploded in his right shoulder. Despite the serious injury it caused, he still managed to safely land his plane back at Getafe. And thus he earned his £1000 injury bonus.

On the evening he met Cox in that small Basque restaurant in Madrid he was still recuperating. After that his role changed to that of trainer, putting Spanish Republican pilots through their paces. He returned to New Zealand in 1937.

Elsewhere in Madrid, another New Zealander was putting his life on the line to fight fascism. Cromwell-born surgeon Douglas Jolly had volunteered to work as a medic. As an Otago University student, Jolly had became involved in the Student Christian Movement, a group that held strong anti-fascist views.

When war broke out in Spain, Jolly hastily abandoned his surgical studies in London. He was given the rank of lieutenant and was attached to the XI International Brigade on the outskirts of Madrid. His twelve-person mobile surgical unit was poorly equipped and under constant pressure but still managed to save many lives. And not just Republican ones. 'I operated on many Italian and German pilots who had been brought down, and on a few Moors,' he wrote later.

After nine months of rescue work in Madrid's battlefields, Jolly was transferred to the front of a Republican offensive in Aragon, where he risked his life alongside the fighters. His team established field hospitals as they went and developed many new tactics in warfare medicine that soon became standard practice, such as establishing blood banks to allow mobile blood transfusions.

For two years solid, Jolly worked saving lives, stitching wounds and setting bones. Along with all other foreign volunteers Jolly left Spain in 1938. His experience during the war made him one of the most experienced battlefield surgeons in Europe—a role that would prove valuable for his fellow New Zealanders in the coming world war.

While Eric Griffiths was flying sorties for the International Squadron and Doug Jolly was mending wounded combatants, Geoffrey Cox continued to write about the war. Two days after he arrived, the bulk of the city's international press corps debunked to Valencia. The inexperienced Cox stayed put and shortly afterwards became one of only three English journalists reporting the inside story of the Battle of Madrid.

As Franco's air force bombarded the city, ground fighting continued on its outskirts. There was no safe place. Cox later recalled one near miss: 'One shell burst just ahead of me, throwing me to the ground. My legs for the moment were numb with shock, and I felt anxiously for signs of blood. But there was none, and I completed the last fifty yards to shelter as if I were on a rugby field with the entire All Black pack after me.'

Despite the best efforts of Franco's forces, the Republican stronghold of Madrid didn't fall. Cox returned to Britain in December 1936, expecting to be back in Spain in six weeks. It wasn't to be—the newspaper decided to send more senior reporters. But Cox continued his efforts to share the horrors of the civil war with the world. He wrote a book, *Defence of Madrid*, vividly describing his experiences during the siege of the city.

Cox went on to cover the rise of Nazism in Europe—breaking the news of Germany's invasion of France in 1939—before fleeing through Bordeaux upon the fall of France to join the New Zealand Army in World War II. He fought at Monte Cassino and ended up as chief intelligence officer for General Bernard Freyberg in Crete.

He was twice mentioned in dispatches and made a military MBE. After the war he returned to England to forge a distinguished journalistic career, for which he received a knighthood in 1966. He died in 2008, five days short of his 98th birthday. He always regarded his experiences in Spain as among the most significant in his life.

Sir Keith Park

Battler of Britain

It wasn't a good start to the day. Keith Park, commander of London's air defence in the Battle of Britain, realised over breakfast that he'd forgotten his wife's birthday. 'Never mind,' she said cheerily, 'a good bag of German aircraft would be an excellent present.'

Dol Park knew her husband had other things on his mind. He was the Thames boy who had served as a corporal in the New Zealand army at Gallipoli in World War I before joining the British air force and working his way up to air vice marshal. It was 15 September 1940 and for two months the Luftwaffe had been pounding bombs on London and south-east England—the very areas Park was charged with protecting. He was under immense pressure, not just from the immediate threat of the German onslaught, but also from many of his peers in the senior British ranks.

Several fellow air commanders were harshly critical of Park's tactic of sending out waves of small squadrons to meet the invading German aircraft instead of fewer large formations. He believed the larger contingents took too long to assemble and were comparatively hard to control. The smaller squadrons enabled the RAF to respond quickly and flexibly, ration their scarce resources and keep fresh reinforcements in reserve to meet further waves of attack.

The internal politics had become so bitter that a week earlier, on 7 September, Park had been tied up in a tense conference away from his underground headquarters in London's Uxbridge when the Germans surprised the city with a massive daylight attack, involving 300 bombers. Park, who commanded 23 fighter squadrons and more than 250 planes, was renowned for his innate ability to sense the enemy's plans and quickly and calmly deploy his squadrons to thwart them. Though his Number 11 Group of defenders fought valiantly, London was hit hard without him in the operations room.

When Park finally escaped from the meeting he returned to his base to give instructions then climbed into his own Hurricane to survey the fiery damage. A former ace fighter pilot, the 48-year-old was one of the few commanders of his rank and age who made a point of keeping up their flying hours so they were still able to man the front line.

That night the Luftwaffe returned, terrorising the city for seven hours, their paths lit by the fires their bombs had started in daylight. It was the heaviest bombardment the country had then sustained and, though the British forces shot down more aircraft than they lost, the outnumbered RAF struggled to defend the city.

Earlier that day the Air Ministry had become so resigned to a German land invasion that it had ordered Park to demolish every airfield in south-east England. He'd refused to carry out the order, fearing that such a move would leave the country defenceless and turn an invasion from a possibility into an inevitability.

After that terrifying night there was a lull of sorts. The Germans had evidently put everything they had into the attack and needed time to recuperate. Park took the opportunity to revise some of his group's tactics. No longer would they fly in V-shaped formations of three aircraft; they would fly in looser formations of four, which would give them a better collective view of the sky and put them in a stronger position to defend each other. Park sensed another attack was imminent and readied his squadrons.

Sure enough, even as he was sitting down to breakfast with his wife, the Germans were launching what they hoped would be the decisive day in their quest to overcome Britain's air defences. And so it would prove, but not in the way they had intended.

That morning, Park had received intelligence that German forces were preparing for another big assault. A large formation of aircraft was reported to be crossing the Channel. In Park's operations bunker, all eyes were on the markers on the map table, which were being updated as radar reports came in. Among the observers in the bunker that day was British Prime Minister Winston Churchill.

Churchill was at first uncharacteristically quiet as he watched Park. Then he broke his silence: 'There appear to be many aircraft coming in.' It was an understatement. More than 200 German bombers had by then been reported leaving the coast of France. Park responded with typical calm: 'And we are ready for them. There'll be someone there to meet them.'

As the reports came in, Park scrambled his waiting squadrons. The prime minister later recalled Park 'watching with vigilant eye every move in the game . . . and only occasionally intervening with some decisive order, usually to reinforce a threatened area'. Churchill knew that the country's fate largely depended on Park and Group 11, and he evidently had confidence in the New Zealander, who had already distinguished himself in leading the withdrawal from Dunkirk earlier that year. 'All the daylight actions in the south of England had already been conducted by him, and all his arrangements and apparatus had been brought to the highest perfection,' Churchill had said.

Churchill's faith in Park was so strong that a visit to the bunker had inspired one of his most famous speeches, made only weeks earlier: 'Never in the field of human conflict was so much owed by so many to so few.' Park was one of the few.

It was a fierce battle, but Park's careful preparations and his new tactics were mercilessly effective. Luftwaffe gunner Hans

Zonderlind later remembered being under extreme pressure from the time his squadron reached England, all the way to the outskirts of London.

'The British fighters had been with us since we had first crossed the English coast and had gathered in intensity all the time. Our escort had been doing a grand job with the Spitfires at keeping them away from us, and we thought that should things remain like this, then this bombing run would be made easy.

'We saw the Hurricanes coming towards us and it seemed that the whole of the RAF was there; we had never seen so many British fighters coming at us at once. I saw a couple of our comrades go down, and we got hit once but it did no great damage. All around us were dogfights as the fighters went after each other, then as we were getting ready for our approach to the target, we saw what must have been a hundred RAF fighters coming at us. We thought that this must have been all the RAF planes up at once, but where were they coming from? We had been told that the RAF fighters were very close to extinction.

'We could not keep our present course, we turned to starboard and did all that we could to avoid the fighters and after a while I am sure we had lost our bearings, so we just dropped our bombs and made our retreat.'

It was a typical scenario. Park's men, reinforced by squadrons from neighbouring commands, largely broke up each raid before it reached its target. Even on retreat there was no let-up for the limping German aircraft–Park had fighters ready to pick them off on their way home.

London still sustained plenty of damage, especially in the south, but because the Luftwaffe formations were so effectively broken by the defending aircraft, they were left scrambling to drop bombs wherever they could. Their eventual targets were too random to be strategically effective.

Legendary RAF squadron leader Douglas Bader later recalled: 'This time, for a change, we outnumbered the Hun . . . At one time you could see planes going down on fire all over the place, and the sky seemed full of parachutes. It was sudden death that morning, for our fighters shot them to blazes.'

Thanks mainly to Park and his pilots, it was such a disastrous day for Germany that Nazi leader Adolf Hitler decided to postpone his planned full-scale invasion of Britain—never getting a chance to reschedule it. Though the Luftwaffe continued to pelt bombs on the UK for another two months, 15 September is remembered as the day the battle was won, and is now commemorated as Battle of Britain Day.

Unfortunately for Park, the successes of that day didn't put the internal squabbling within senior military command to rest. Though many of his controversial tactics had been proved effective, he was relieved of his command within three months. It would be years before his contribution to the Battle of Britain was recognised.

His biographer, Vincent Orange, wrote: 'Week after week, throughout the whole campaign, Park showed uncommon strength of mind in resisting pressure from both senior and junior officers to use larger forces than he thought proper. That resistance cost him his job once the battle was over.'

Park was exiled to a training role in Gloucestershire. But he was redeployed shortly afterwards to the small but vital strategic post of Malta, where he was made commander of the RAF base. He further distinguished himself in the Siege of Malta and was knighted in 1942. In early 1944 he was promoted to air marshal and made RAF commander for the Middle East, then for South-East Asia. In December 1946 he retired, with the rank of air chief marshal, and later returned to New Zealand.

Two months after his return, the head of the RAF, Lord Tedder, made a speech about Park that finally recognised his efforts: 'If ever any one man won the Battle of Britain, he did. I don't believe it is realised how much that one man, with his leadership, his calm judgment and his skill, did to save not only this country, but the world.'

When Park died in 1975, the British government declared he was a man 'whose name will stand in the roll of honour of defenders of freedom for all time'. At a memorial service in London, airman Douglas Bader—who had been one of Park's detractors during the Battle of Britain—was eager to put the matter to rights. He acknowledged in a eulogy that Park had controlled the battle and brought it to a successful conclusion. 'The awesome responsibility for this country's survival rested squarely on Keith Park's shoulders.'

After a long campaign by Park's admirers, who had dubbed him London's neglected hero, it was announced in 2009 that a bronze statue of him would be erected in Waterloo Place, London. Perhaps appropriately, considering Park's World War II experience, intense political wrangling and public controversy denied the statue a more prominent spot on a plinth in Trafalgar Square.

Charles Upham

New Zealand's bravest soldier

Lieutenant Charles Upham had a bullet in his ankle, one arm in a sling from a shrapnel wound and such a bad case of dysentery that he'd hardly been able to eat. Sleep was a distant memory. But there was one more great challenge ahead before he and his comrades could escape from what had become a disastrous battle.

It was 30 May 1941 and the Battle of Crete was coming to a humiliating end for the overpowered Allied troops. In ten days the Germans had overrun the island, which was a key strategic post in the Mediterranean.

The fighting hadn't been all one-sided. Though the Germans held out in the end, an estimated 4000 of their troops had died, slightly more than the Allied toll of 3600. Another 12,000 British, Australian and New Zealand soldiers had been captured.

One of Upham's last tasks in a dramatic tour of duty on the island had been to secure the 65-kilometre Allied escape route through the island's interior to a little fishing village called Sphakia on the south coast. The withdrawal had been a pitiful sight. Even the men who'd managed to avoid the rain of bullets and shrapnel were wasted and drawn from lack of food, water and sleep. And for thousands the only viable mode of transport along the long, hilly escape route was their own weary legs.

Now at the village, the exhausted men were hiding in caves and gullies and waiting for nightfall, when the British Navy would

Huria Matenga braved enormous seas near Nelson in September 1863 to help save the crew of a shipwrecked brigatine. The only public remark she ever made was: 'It was nothing.'

Sea captain Frank Worsley joined explorer Ernest Shackleton's 1914–1916 expedition to the Antarctic but his ship was caught in ice and crushed. He led 28 men in three lifeboats to an island, before setting out in a tiny boat in huge seas to get help.

A photographer stands on the remains of the rail bridge at Tangiwai, which washed away in a flood in 1954, sending a train hurtling into the swollen river. Though 151 people died, the courageous actions of crew, passengers and passersby saved dozens of lives.

The Wahine ferry founders in Wellington Harbour after striking a reef during a cyclone in 1968. Its 734 passengers and crew were hurriedly evacuated and hundreds of locals rushed in to rescue them from the rough seas. Their combined efforts saved 683 lives.

Ngapuhi chief Hone Heke fought tirelessly against British colonial repression of Maori in the 1830s and 1840s. His most famous act was chopping down the flagpole carrying the Union Jack at Kororareka, then the seat of colonial power.

As a commander during the battle of Gallipoli in World War I, Colonel William Malone was renowned for his determination, drive and ability to impose order among the chaos. He was killed at Chunuk Bair in August 1915.

Shouldering heavy pressure and harsh criticism, World War II air commander Sir Keith Park stood firm in his unconventional tactics to successfully defend London from the Luftwaffe. He earned the praise of British Prime Minister, Sir Winston Churchill.

Captain Charles Upham became the most highly decorated Commonwealth soldier of World War II. His citation commended his 'superb coolness, great skill and dash'. Upham is pictured here with Major-General Sir Howard Kippenberger, a renowned New Zealand military leader.

Wellington-born Nancy Wake parachuted into occupied France during World War II as a British undercover agent. She ended up leading a band of resistance fighters and became the most decorated Allied servicewoman.

Lance Corporal Willie Apiata received the Victoria Cross for carrying a wounded comrade to safety after an ambush by insurgents in Afghanistan in 2004. He said he was 'only doing my job' but was officially cited for demonstrating 'the highest order of personal courage under fire'.

be able to risk ferrying them out. But it appeared the enemy was keen to pick through them one more time. From a ravine nearby came the sound of gunfire. Through binoculars, a brigadier spotted a platoon of advancing Germans.

'Well, we've had it now,' muttered another officer. 'They've caught us. This looks like the finish.'

New Zealand battalion commander Lieutenant-Colonel (later Major-General) Howard Kippenberger wasn't giving up so easily. He summoned his company leaders and briefed them.

Shortly afterwards Captain Den Fountaine, the officer in charge of C Company, ran up to Upham, one of his platoon commanders. 'Get your men up there, Charlie!' he said, pointing to the dizzyingly steep 200-metre-high cliffs on the western side of the ravine. 'Get on top of them. And you'd better move fast. They're in a hell of a flap at Force HQ.'

Upham, a sheep farmer and valuer from Canterbury, managed a weary grin. 'Oh, tell 'em to go to hell and not get excited.' He turned to his right-hand man, Sergeant Dave Kirk, and said, 'Get the boys moving, Dave. And tell 'em it's a five-minute job.'

In fact, the slog up the cliffs by Upham and his men took two hours. Ignoring his injuries and illness, Upham kept pushing higher and higher, aware that the steeper the angle at which they opened fire, the more chance they had of succeeding.

Corporal W. H. Vincent of C Company, who was watching from below, later recalled: 'The going was hard and the men were very tired, but, led by Lieutenant Upham, they toiled up the steep slope until they observed Germans running between rhododendron bushes in the bed of the ravine, which was otherwise devoid of cover.'

Finally, Upham stopped climbing. 'This'll do.' The platoon swiftly readied their Bren gun. The sides of the ravine were so steep that one of the men had to be held by the legs so that he could lean over far enough to fire.

‘Right,’ said Upham. ‘Let her go!’

The soldiers waiting anxiously in the ravine at last heard a sharp burst of gunfire. ‘It lasted about a minute, there were then some single shots, and then silence,’ recalled a watching soldier. ‘A little later Upham’s platoon started to come back and then a message came that all of the enemy party had been killed, completely helpless under his plunging fire.’

In fact Upham had at one point taken the gun to personally finish off the attackers. Once he’d stopped firing they’d waited a minute, then he’d said, simply: ‘That’s the lot.’ He was later credited with killing 22 Germans at a distance of 500 metres and forcing the rest to flee.

It was one of several skirmishes in the nine-day Battle of Crete that earned Charles Upham the Victoria Cross, the highest military decoration in the Commonwealth.

Despite his offer to stay behind and continue fighting, his commanding officers ordered him to evacuate that night, aware that he was ignoring his own need for medical attention. He was barely aboard the Navy ship before his exploits started turning into legend, as the men who’d witnessed them began to swap tales. It wasn’t long before every New Zealand soldier in Europe had heard of Charles Upham.

One of his platoon troops on Crete, Private Melville Hill-Rennie, later described in detail a firefight Upham had taken control of:

‘A Jerry machine-gun nest opened fire on us at a range of 50 yards and they got four of our boys before we could drop to the ground . . . We edged forward on our stomachs until we were within 20 yards of the Nazis, who were tucked away behind a large tree, and then opened fire with our one Tommy gun, one Bren gun and eight rifles.

‘As we kept up the fire the platoon officer [Upham] cautiously crawled round to the side and slightly to the rear of the tree.

Although it was still dark, we could tell by the way the Jerries were shouting to each other that they didn't like the look of the situation. When he got round behind the tree the platoon officer jumped to his feet and hurled three Mills bombs, one right after another, into the nest and then jumped forward with his revolver blazing. Single-handed he wiped out seven Jerries with their Tommy guns and another with a machine gun.

'We pushed on slowly for another 50 yards or so. By this time it was getting light and I could make out the shape of a house on the edge of the road just ahead. Just then Jerry opened up with machine guns from the windows of the house and from a small outhouse at the rear. We fell to the ground again and took cover.

'I got a bead on one of the windows and as soon as one of the Nazis poked his head above the sill with his machine gun I let fly . . . [Upham] dashed ahead again and came around from the back towards the door of the outhouse. "Come on out," he shouted. Jerry's answer was a burst of fire. Taking a Mills bomb from his pocket [Upham] calmly pulled the catch then carefully placed it into the hand of a dead Jerry whose arm was stretched out through the outhouse door.

'"Take that, you b–s," I heard him say; then he stepped back and waited for the explosion. As soon as the bomb went off he shouted, "Come on, boys, they're finished," and we rushed forward.

'We slowly blasted our way from house to house, wiping out one nest after another, while the snipers kept up a constant, deadly fire. At one house the Nazis had mounted a captured British Bofors gun from the aerodrome behind a well and were turning it on our men with devastating results. We just had to wipe out that gun crew.

'With two Bren gunners I sneaked forward until I was in a position to cover [Upham] who crawled forward on his stomach for 30 yards; then he tossed his Mills bomb smack onto a gunner crouched behind the wall.'

On another occasion Upham was wounded in the shoulder by shrapnel. He ordered Sergeant Kirk to extract it with a pocket knife, rather than desert his men to go to the aid post. This was classic Upham. Shortly afterwards he took a ricocheted bullet in his ankle, which he put up with for two weeks before digging it out himself when the wound began to fester.

In one incident he pretended to be dead as two Germans approached him to finish him off. He waited until they were standing right over him then sprang around and shot both of them dead with his rifle–even with one arm in a sling from the earlier shrapnel injury.

In yet another skirmish, when he found himself surrounded by the enemy, he ordered his platoon to stay hidden while he paraded up and down in full view, to draw enemy fire so his men could pinpoint and attack the German positions. 'There Charlie was,' Corporal 'Keg' McKegney later recalled, 'telling us to keep down, keep down, and all the time standing there in the open himself, his arm in a sling . . . [He wandered] around as if it didn't matter, lead flying everywhere.'

Upham's official citation for the Victoria Cross commends him for 'a series of remarkable exploits, showing outstanding leadership, tactical skill and utter indifference to danger . . . He showed superb coolness, great skill and dash. His conduct and leadership inspired his whole platoon to fight magnificently throughout, and in fact was an inspiration to the battalion.'

But Charlie Upham's war was far from over. He was moved on to the Middle East and promoted to captain. Within two months he became one of only three people ever to earn a Victoria Cross and Bar (technically, that means he earned two Victoria Crosses).

The second honour was for another series of gallant acts, over a three-week period during which he was wounded three times. In one attack he was shot in the elbow by a machine-gun bullet and his arm was broken. The citation reads: 'He stayed with his men until the objective was captured and until positions were consolidated. He reported to the RAP [aid station] and then, with his arm in splints, went back to his Company and stayed with it all day under the most trying conditions of heavy enemy artillery and mortar fire. The enemy made a strong counter-attack late in the afternoon, and Captain Upham was again wounded by mortar fire. He was no longer able to walk. Captain Upham was taken prisoner of war on 15 July 1942 . . .

'He showed fine leadership at all times and under his command his Company earned a remarkable reputation in attack. Captain Upham's complete indifference to danger and his personal bravery has become a byword in the whole of the New Zealand Expeditionary Force.'

Upham was 33 when he was captured—and proceeded to make himself a nightmare prisoner. After numerous escape attempts from Italian and German prisoner-of-war camps he was locked up in the notorious Colditz prison in Germany in 1944. He remained there until the Americans liberated it on 15 April 1945. In true Upham style, upon being freed he immediately acquired an American army uniform, fully prepared to fight on, but was ordered back to England.

There's a romantic post-script to Upham's tour of duty. As soon as he arrived in England, he tried to find Molly McTamney, a nurse he'd fallen in love with at the races in Christchurch ten years earlier. He was told she was working in Germany for the Red Cross and immediately made plans to return to the country he'd spent almost three years trying to escape. But she raced back to England to find him first. She was amused that since they'd met he'd become a legend. His letters and postcards to her during the war had been so placid and homely she'd wondered if he was the same man who was in all the newspapers.

On 11 May 1945 she joined him at Buckingham Palace to see King George IV pin the VC on him. A month later they were married in a quiet ceremony at New Milton in Hampshire.

Upham was overwhelmed to be received as a national hero upon his return to New Zealand. In a speech to a civic reception held in Christchurch in his honour, he credited his success to his fellow soldiers:

'There were thousands of better soldiers than I was. In the army, as you all know, everything is cut and dried—already planned by someone else—and carried out by the people underneath. The only way to get things done was by taking risks, and those who took the risks were those who did not come back.'

Upham lived out his life quietly, mostly as a sheep farmer in North Canterbury. He died in Christchurch in November 1994.

Nancy Wake

Femme fatale of the French Resistance

The Gestapo officers barely looked up as the well-dressed dark-haired French woman cycled up to their roadblock near the town of Chateauroux in central France. She slowed and reached into her coat as if about to pull out her identity papers, but the Germans casually waved her on.

It was mid-1944, a crucial time in the German occupation of France in World War II. The Allied invasion of Normandy had begun in the north but thousands of Nazi troops were stuck waging a fierce battle against guerilla armies in the centre of the country. A harmless young housewife was of no consequence.

But the heart in the cyclist's chest was pounding far harder than a mere bike ride warranted. Had the guards been more alert they might have discovered that she had no papers. She was in fact Nancy Wake, a 31-year-old Wellington-born, Australian-raised operative for the British Special Operations Service who had become a leader of the French guerilla movement and had earned a spot high on the Gestapo's most-wanted list. And she was on an epic mission that would help to secure the Resistance's hold on the region and send the German occupiers fleeing.

Since parachuting in from England several months earlier, in late March 1944, Wake had been stationed with a local guerilla army, one of the legendary Maquis bands that made up the quasi-military arm of the French Resistance. The only woman among

7000 men, she had quickly earned a reputation for fighting hard and drinking hard, and had proved herself a natural leader.

Wake was a key decision-maker and fighter in the Maquis' day-to-day guerilla operations against the Nazis—throwing grenades with the best of them—but she also had the crucial job of directing the supply of arms, cash, clothing and other equipment from London. Without the nocturnal parachute drops she organised, the passionate but strongly outnumbered Maquis would be helpless against the Germans. With her help they were lethal.

By mid-1944 Wake and her team had developed a smooth system. She would work with a Maquis radio operator to order supplies from London, directing British planes to drop them by night in fields, and then she would lead a team to round up the parcels and distribute them. The impact of her work cannot be overstated—it enabled the Resistance to boost its efforts in central France and keep German reinforcements from getting to the front lines in Normandy.

But then disaster struck. Wake's radio operator became surrounded by Germans during a particularly fierce skirmish and, following protocol, he abandoned his equipment and codes. Though injured, he managed to at least bury the crucial tools so the enemy couldn't find them.

The man eventually escaped but the loss of the radio and codes left the Maquis with a big problem. Though they were proving to be an incredibly effective force—taking big German casualties for minimal sacrifices—without a constant supply of firepower they were vulnerable. They needed another radio. And to get one they needed to send an urgent message to London—via a radio.

With tens of thousands of Germans patrolling the area, their options were limited. There was another radio operator in the village of Chateauroux, some 200 kilometres from their modest headquarters, but they couldn't possibly saunter up there in a car—that would immediately raise the suspicion of the Gestapo, who had set up roadblocks everywhere.

So Wake decided their best chance was to send the most innocuous-looking member of the Maquis—herself—by bike, dressed as a French housewife who might just be riding into the nearest village for groceries.

First she had to look the part. Though she was famous for prioritising personal grooming while hiding out for months in the wilderness—even wearing make-up and sleeping in a frilly nightgown with a satin cushion for a pillow—her clothes were ripped and dirty. And a woman wearing trousers, as Wake tended to, would automatically raise suspicion.

The first part of the plan involved Wake patching and cleaning herself up as best she could and cycling into a nearby village to get measured for a respectable outfit. Even this was noticed almost immediately by the Gestapo—while she was waiting for the clothes to be made she received a message from the tailor warning her that the Germans had been asking questions.

So she returned to collect the suit disguised as the daughter of a local peasant. In borrowed dowdy clothes, a severe hairstyle and no make-up, and riding in the back of a horse-drawn cart filled with vegetables, she didn't warrant a second glance from the German soldiers, even though the cart was stopped more than a dozen times on the 20 minute journey. Even the tailor didn't immediately recognise her.

The following day she set off in her new outfit. She was unarmed—she figured she had more chance of talking herself out of trouble with her flawless French than shooting her way out. She had no documentation, even though it was compulsory to carry identity papers (hers were out-of-date and she couldn't risk getting new ones) and bicycle licence papers.

The risk was enormous. She was a wanted woman entering heavily occupied territory. She had a price on her head for earlier exploits with the Resistance—smuggling messages and food, slipping away from would-be captors and manning an escape network for Allied soldiers and Jewish soldiers (before fleeing across the Pyrenees to Spain herself in mid-1943). She didn't know it then, but her beloved French husband, Henri Fiocca, had already been captured and tortured by German interrogators desperate to find the elusive woman they'd dubbed 'the white mouse'.

Wherever possible she stuck to country lanes—making the journey even longer. When she had to take main roads she would push the bike so she could quickly duck aside and hide if a German car approached. She met up with contacts who warned her of spots to steer clear of; she dined in bistros, ears straining for gossip about German movements; she drank a publican under the table to extract information; she slept briefly in a barn under a heap of straw; she bought vegetables and slung them in a string bag from the bicycle to complement her disguise; she stopped frequently to freshen up.

'It was absolutely imperative,' she later told Australian journalist Peter Fitzsimons, 'that even though I was exhausted and windblown from travelling so far, I should not look that way. Whatever German patrols saw me had to think I was simply a young housewife tootling along home or to the village, who was not worth bothering with, but not someone doing a major trip.'

Many times it was impossible to avoid the numerous Germans. On these occasions she would simply pedal casually through the middle of them. Sometimes truckloads of Germans would pass her and call out. She would wave demurely back, though, she said later, 'I longed to break their f-ing necks.'

If she approached a checkpoint she would flutter her eyelashes and make a coquettish joke of it—'Do you want to search me?' Fortunately, without fail they declined, laughed, and waved her by.

By the time she reached Chateauroux she had been pedalling for

30 of the previous 39 hours, through mostly mountainous terrain. She was exhausted and her legs felt like they were on fire. But there was a bigger challenge ahead. Her contact, a fellow undercover officer working for the British, didn't believe her story or her identity. And she didn't have the requisite secret codes that would identify her—they had died with a colleague before he'd had a chance to pass them on. The contact refused to let her use his radio.

Luckily, she bumped into a friendly face—a Maquis fighter whose unit had also lost its radio, along with the operator, and who was in Chateauroux on the same mission. He had come in search of a French radio operator in the town. But he and Wake quickly discovered that the man had fled. They were warned that the Gestapo was hiding in his house to catch anyone who came knocking. It was a lucky escape, but it got them no nearer their goal.

'The town was literally swarming with Germans,' recalled Wake in her autobiography. 'They were completely surrounding areas and checking the houses systematically, so we decided to leave immediately. We separated and arranged to meet outside the town.'

Wake's new companion had one more trick up his sleeve—he knew of a Maquis group hiding out in a nearby area. It meant another 50 kilometres of pedalling, but Wake didn't hesitate. This time they were successful: the message was sent to London, via the Free French army in Algeria.

Relieved, Wake set off home, recklessly abandoning many of the precautions she'd taken on the outward journey. 'Every kilometre I pedalled was sheer agony. I knew that if I ever got off the bike I could never get on it again, so I kept pedalling.'

By the time Wake made it back, she'd pedalled 500 kilometres in 72 hours. 'All I could do was cry. When I got off that damned bike I felt as if I had a fire between my legs, and the inside of my thighs were raw. I couldn't stand up, I couldn't sit down, I couldn't walk and I didn't sleep for days. But thanks to all the help I had been given by one and all, I had succeeded . . . When I'm asked what I'm most proud of doing during the war, I say "the bike ride".'

London came through. Not only did they send a new radio within 48 hours, but a spare radio operator and, subsequently, two American weapons instructors with a full load of bazookas. The bazookas were immediately put to good use to foil an attack by 500 crack German troops on Wake's camp of 115 fighters. Without the superior weaponry secured by Wake's two-wheeled quest, the Maquis would have been done for.

Wake spent the rest of the war generally messing up German plans. On one occasion she even put her hand-to-hand combat training to the test by killing a German guard with a karate-like chop to the neck—but not before sustaining a nasty gash from his bayonet.

On another mission, she joined in a lunchtime raid on the German headquarters in Montluçon—sneaking in the back door, running up the stairs and tossing a grenade into the lunch room before fleeing in a getaway car. 'Several dozen Germans did not lunch that day, nor any other day for that matter,' she later wrote.

As the war drew to a close, Wake was devastated to discover that her husband had been executed by the Nazis on 16 October 1943, after refusing to give them any information about her. Heartbroken, she blamed herself for his death. Exactly a year later she flew back to London, her mission very much accomplished.

She was adorned with a chestful of medals, making her the most decorated Allied servicewoman ever. Her accolades included the British George Medal, the American Medal of Freedom and several sought-after French honours, including the Medaille de la Resistance and the Croix de Guerre with two palms and a star. Her efforts weren't officially recognised in Australia until 2004, when she was made Companion of the Order of Australia. The New

Zealand Returned Services Association in 2006 awarded her its highest honour, the Badge in Gold.

New Zealand still hasn't given her an official honour because, as former Prime Minister Helen Clark said in 2007, 'The connection with New Zealand is extremely tenuous. Apart from being here for a tiny time as a baby she has never lived here.'

Wake's supporters say she still identifies herself as a New Zealander, and carries a New Zealand passport.

At the time of writing, Wake was in her late nineties and living in a rest home in England. She has been quoted saying that when she dies she wants her ashes dropped from a plane over the French mountains she defended.

Willie Apiata

SAS hardman

The first Lance Corporal Willie Apiata knew of the rocket-propelled grenade was when it blasted him out of his sleeping bag. He found himself standing, dazed, beside the four-wheel drive vehicle he had been lying on, his sleeping bag around his ankles and his gear scattered.

The vehicle was blazing in the pitch black Afghanistan night and was being peppered with machine gun and rifle fire from several directions. He didn't know it then, but 20 enemy fighters had crept out of nowhere for the 3.15 a.m. ambush on his patrol of New Zealand SAS soldiers. The Kiwis were outnumbered.

Quickly Apiata ducked behind the vehicle, with a fellow soldier. As the bullets whizzed past he said, 'Where's our man?', referring to a corporal who had been sleeping on the ground nearby. No sooner had he uttered the words than his mate came 'flopping' around the corner of the car.

'I could see he was seriously injured. I could hear it,' Apiata later told his biographer, Paul Little. 'You could turn a tap on right now and hear the water hitting the sink—that was the sound of his blood pouring out and hitting the ground. I don't know what tore through his arm, but it was a massive wound.'

Apiata could see the blast had opened up a major artery in his friend's arm. The other soldier, who had also been wounded by shrapnel, though not as seriously, reached for one of the field dressings that were taped to the outside of the car. In doing so he cast a shadow and the striking militants unleashed their weapons, adding more rocket-propelled grenades to their assault. The blazing vehicle had become the perfect target in the desert night. To make matters worse, the men and their vehicle were stranded between the enemy and their own main contingent, hindering their colleagues' ability to return fire. 'You could feel every round ripping through the vehicle,' said Apiata later. 'I'm amazed he made it.'

The two soldiers quickly did what they could to stem the injured man's blood flow. But he was lapsing in and out of consciousness, and Apiata knew that unless they got him to a medic immediately his mate was done for. And the medic was with the rest of the patrol, 70 metres away, across open, rocky ground alive with bullets and grenades. Apiata knew there was no possibility of getting the help to come to them under such heavy fire. They had to get to the main troop position.

When one of the patrol's other vehicles roared out and, from inside, a soldier unleashed a long burst of machine gun fire on the attackers, Apiata saw his chance. 'We're out of here–we gotta go,' he said.

'When we started,' he recalled later, 'I had my injured mate's arm over my shoulder, but he was in so much shock and had lost so much blood he couldn't walk. He went only about five or ten paces, perhaps not even that. And then he collapsed. We were out in the open at this stage, with firing going on all around us, so I picked him up and put him on my shoulder.'

Apiata had to shrug off his Army training, which had taught him to stay low to avoid bullets, in favour of going at speed.

There was, one of his fellow soldiers reported later, 'a shitload of stuff coming towards them–rocket-propelled grenades, machine gun fire, small arms fire. There were explosions everywhere, and they were caught in the middle. How they got through we will never know.'

Accompanied by the third soldier who'd been sheltering behind the car, Apiata ran up the hill with the injured man on his back, and called out to the medic. When the man appeared, he said, 'Look after our mate.'

While the medic took over, Apiata grabbed a spare machine gun and a big link of ammunition, ran to the spot from where his fellow soldiers were firing, and, in his words, 'got into it'.

After about 20 minutes the enemy combatants fled, leaving behind several of their dead. Apiata's mate was flown to a hospital in Germany and survived. Medical staff said he probably would have died of blood loss and shock if Apiata hadn't got him to the medic as quickly as he did.

Later, Apiata told Little that he'd suffered 'just a scratch' in the encounter. 'I can't explain why I didn't get hit. None of us did when we were crossing that hill through the fire. My mate didn't get hit when he was on my back and the other guy didn't get hit. It's a miracle we made it. Everyone could see us coming in the light from the burning vehicle. All the weapons firing lit up the area even more.'

Because of the secrecy that surrounds the operations of the SAS, New Zealand's elite Army force, no details have been released of where in Afghanistan the firefight took place, or even on what date in 2004. The names of the injured man and the third soldier have also been kept a secret.

Later, Apiata's troop commander, who'd witnessed his bravery on that night, told Apiata he was going to put his name forward for a medal.

Apiata declined.

'It's not going to be a Victoria Cross or anything,' said the commander. 'But you deserve a medal.'

Three years later Apiata stood at attention inside Government House in Wellington and received the New Zealand Victoria Cross from the Governor-General, Anand Satyanand. He was the first person to be awarded the Victoria Cross for New Zealand, the new New Zealand version of the traditional British Empire medal. He was also the first New Zealander awarded the Victoria Cross since World War II, and is one of only about a dozen living recipients worldwide. Two other soldiers received bravery awards for their actions during the same incident, but were not named for security reasons.

Apiata's citation reads, in part: 'As the enemy pressed its attack towards Lance Corporal Apiata's position, and without thought of abandoning his colleague to save himself, he took a decision in the highest order of personal courage under fire. Knowing the risks involved in moving to open ground, Lance Corporal Apiata decided to carry Corporal D single-handedly to the relative safety of the main Troop position . . .

'In total disregard of his own safety, Lance Corporal Apiata stood up and lifted his comrade bodily. He then carried him across the seventy metres of broken, rocky and fire swept ground, fully exposed in the glare of battle to heavy enemy fire and into the face of returning fire from the main Troop position. That neither he nor his colleague were hit is scarcely possible. Having delivered his wounded companion to relative shelter with the remainder of the patrol, Lance Corporal Apiata re-armed himself and rejoined the fight in counter-attack.'

Apiata was evidently taken aback by the storm of public attention that accompanied the award. At a press conference in Wellington he said little about the incident, other than that he was 'only doing my job and looking after my mates . . . I was doing what I was trained for.' It's a line he's repeated countless times since.

Accolades flowed in for the softly spoken soldier and a bronze statue of him was quickly commissioned for the lobby of SAS headquarters in Papakura, South Auckland. New Zealand Army chief Major General Lou Gardiner said Apiata was a role model. 'He's a humble, self-effacing good Kiwi bloke who did it for his mates.'

The Prime Minister at the time, Helen Clark, said the soldier had displayed stunning courage. 'He could have saved his own life but he elected to save another person's. It is a miracle that both of them weren't killed in the incident. It brings a lump to the throat to hear of something like this.'

3.

CRUSADERS

Mary Ann Colclough
Kate Sheppard

Pioneering feminists

With tears in his eyes, the Auckland man offloaded his domestic woes to his friend:

'I can't for the life of me tell you what has come over Emma. You know that we have always lived at home most happily until the other day; in fact Emma and I never knew what it was to differ. Now she sits and mopes or cries half the day at a stretch.

'I can't bear to see her miserable, but know of no remedy, for when I ask her what is the matter she only sobs, and says she wants her "rights". In vain I ask her what she means, but she either cannot or will not tell me. The poor children, that used to be so fond of us both, now look upon me as a monster who is killing their dear mother.'

The root of the problem, as the friend recounted in the *Hawke's Bay Herald* in July 1871, was that the man had taken his wife to hear a lecture by a woman called Polly Plum.

Polly Plum was the alias for Auckland widow and early feminist Mary Ann Colclough. Colclough, then aged 35, was an outspoken proponent of women's rights who bolted to prominence in the early 1870s with such outlandish ideas as opening up more employment opportunities to women, better educating them, allowing them greater financial independence and giving them the vote.

Colclough, an English-born mother of two, had been left a widow several years earlier but was one of the fortunate few who had been educated well enough to support her family, albeit on a school teacher's meagre salary.

Though she always maintained her marriage had been a happy one, her husband had been hopeless with financial matters and had spent 'pounds and pounds' of her earnings in profitless and even ruinous speculations.

'I was the breadwinner,' she once wrote, 'whilst he had all the breadwinner's powers and privileges.'

On one occasion, she later recalled, all the 'little home comforts' she had gathered around her by 'unremitting toil' were seized, leaving her and her two children, then both aged under two, on the bare floor. Yet throughout their married life her husband had the right to claim all his wife's property and earnings.

Colclough's campaign for women's rights began as a war of letters to newspapers. Almost every letter was immediately pounced upon by less liberal letter writers—mostly male—who would declare that women were happy as they were and weren't interested in improving their lot.

In one exchange in January 1871, Colclough wrote under her Polly Plum pseudonym to the Auckland-based *Daily Southern Cross* newspaper decrying the cases of two widows—one a mother of six—who'd apparently been sent to the debtor's jail because of their late husbands' debts:

'It seems to me the greatest social anomaly to forbid women to vote, tie their hands with reference to a choice of employments, prate of their domestic sphere as the only proper one for women, curtail their sphere of usefulness so that it is almost impossible for a self-helpful woman to earn a decent living, and yet, whilst loading her with all these disqualifications, to make her as liable as any man to the pains and penalties of the law.'

Several days later the inevitable reply appeared. A male correspondent going by the alias of Old Practical said he couldn't understand the call for women's rights. 'Are women treated worse than they were formerly? Were our ancestors wrong as to the position in which they placed them?'

Their correspondence, via the paper, continued for months. Then in June of that year Colclough was challenged to cast off the pseudonym and take her cause directly to the people, in the form of a public lecture under the title, 'The Subjection of Woman'. It was a gutsy move at a time when it was scandalous for women to even speak in public, let alone air extremist views.

The *Daily Southern Cross* remarked snidely: 'If earnestness in the cause and a thorough acquaintance with the wants and grievances of the weaker half of humanity can prove of any avail with the "lords of creation" to whom we presume her remarks will be chiefly addressed, we have no doubt the ladies of Auckland will soon be emancipated from their bondage.'

But by the end of her lecture, delivered to a large audience in the Auckland City Hall on 26 June, the newspaper had changed its tone. 'No doubt some attended under the impression that there would be something ridiculous about a lady lecturing,' wrote its reporter, '[but] if any did so, they must have been disappointed. In her manner the lecturer was calm, dignified and impressive. Her matter was good and she had a persuasive style of delivery that evidently was not without its effect on the audience.'

Colclough's talk was wide-ranging: the inadequacy of education for girls, the folly of those who flouted their feminine wares by promenading down Queen Street, the need to make single women more independent, and even that husbands should be more understanding of their wives' concerns: 'The husband should be as ready to chase away the cloud from the wife's brow as she should be to chase the cloud from his. He should be willing to admit that a wet washing day is to her quite as great a worry as a fall in the sharemarket is to him, and that due allowance is to be made for her feeling gloomy about it.'

It was feminism, 1870s-style, and it propelled Colclough from anonymous letter writer to figurehead for the beginnings of the suffrage movement in New Zealand. The success of the lecture led to several more throughout the country—though they were less well attended, perhaps because she had ceased to be a novelty—and she kept up the letter-writing. Though the *Daily Southern Cross* was reasonably supportive, it did eventually make her pay for advertising space to accommodate her frequent letters.

Crucially, she believed girls should be in school from the ages of seven to sixteen, so they could learn to be both capable wives and to be independent. This, she believed, would solve the common problem of widows being left penniless and reliant on charity, and would give purpose to the lives of 'useless females'—those women who never married and had little option but to live off their parents. She called for more professions and trades to be opened up to women, including medicine, and for women to have more self-determination in matters that affected them. She challenged the right of fathers to have sole control of their children and called for the protection of the property of married women. She also pressed for improvements in the working conditions of female labourers—mostly shop assistants, domestics and seamstresses—and an end to female employment in bars.

Colclough's many detractors—including a group of Auckland barmaids—accused her of myriad crimes, from a 'want of modesty' and making women despise their marital duties, to subverting Christianity and trying to destroy the home.

In an extraordinarily long and scathing editorial, the *Evening Post* in Wellington described her as a soured and disappointed old maid (when she complained, they claimed it was a printing error) and called her notorious letters 'wretched twaddle'. The *Taranaki Herald* dismissed her views as 'Yankee ideas'.

But Colclough never tired of following an argument to the bitter end. 'We don't want to be men—or only a few silly ones do,' she wrote in July 1870, 'but we want to be as free as men; and we love our babies too well to neglect them, even supposing there was no real force to bind us to do our husband's will.'

She became frustrated, however, when audiences for her lectures dwindled—not so much because of her views, she believed, but because people wanted to be amused when they went out. She was urged to introduce singing and dancing into her evening programmes.

Perhaps annoyed at her apparent lack of progress in New Zealand, Colclough took her campaign to Melbourne in 1875. There, it appears, she encountered even fiercer opposition.

The Age newspaper reported: 'We are afraid she will not reform the world by her lectures . . . for women as a rule are quite contented with their position, and have no wish to usurp the position of their "Lords and masters".'

In New Zealand, the press reported her apparent failure with none-too-subtle glee. Said the *Auckland Star*: 'We really do not know that Auckland has sustained any serious loss in the absence of this lady, or that Melbourne has won a grand prize in her acquisition.'

The following year Colclough returned to New Zealand, and seems to have quietly returned to teaching. She died in Picton in 1885 from injuries sustained in an accident.

'Mary Colclough was a highly controversial public figure for a few years only,' wrote historian Judith Malone in the *Dictionary of New Zealand Biography*, 'but she jolted the people of Auckland by fundamentally challenging contemporary assumptions and values about woman's place in New Zealand society.'

Though Colclough eventually fell silent, other women had by then taken up many key platforms of her cause, as had several key politicians. Prominent among the women was Kate Sheppard. Sheppard's method was far less confrontational than Colclough's and her campaign was better timed. In the two decades or so between the two women's campaigns, public opinion about women's rights had begun to shift. The first of several defeated bills calling for women's suffrage was presented in the House of Representatives in 1879. Sheppard didn't let the repeated setbacks dim her quiet ambition.

Like Colclough, Sheppard had been born in England, had emigrated to New Zealand with her family in her early twenties and was married a few years later. In her early thirties, while living in her adopted home town of Auckland, she gave birth to a son.

But while Colclough was motivated by her own experiences, Sheppard's campaign appears to have had a more theoretical foundation. Sheppard once said she worked for the women's franchise because she'd given the issue a lot of thought and had studied many books about it. She was galvanised into action by a visit to New Zealand in 1885 of American temperance campaigner Mary Clement Leavitt.

Though Sheppard worked as a journalist she wasn't the main breadwinner in the family so was perhaps less constrained than Colclough had been by the need to earn money and therefore could devote more time to the cause. She too was concerned about education for women, equal opportunities and equal pay but her main motivation was temperance. She quickly discovered that women were powerless to lobby for law changes to lessen the disastrous effects alcohol was having on families and communities. For women to have the political power to push for temperance, they needed the vote.

Like Colclough, Sheppard developed a talent for letter writing and public speaking but her approach was less confrontational. She was careful to alienate neither men nor women, mindful that the majority of women would not want to be associated with a cause that pushed society's boundaries too far. She made clear that the vote would be an extension of a woman's responsibilities within the home, not a threat to them.

In an editorial in March 1893 commenting on an article by Sheppard, the *Hawke's Bay Herald* declared, 'There is nothing of the "Shrieking Sisterhood" style in Mrs Sheppard's paper. It is couched in terse, masculine language, pleasantly tempered by a genial sarcasm, which hits right home but does not wound.'

And those in her target audience were more ready to listen than Colclough's audience had been in 1870—with one notable exception: Richard Seddon, who had just become premier.

Seddon had been a leading opponent of the 1879 suffrage bill, and of every other suffrage bill for the next thirteen years. In 1886 he said, 'I will not have it said that the majority of our members of the House are under petticoat government. We shall have to look to our laurels to assert our prerogative as the Lords of Creation before long . . . I say if you give too much power you unsex women.'

Sheppard and her fellow campaigners kept their cool. And they kept writing, speaking, lobbying and gathering signatures for petitions.

On 19 September 1893 the dogged persistence of Colclough, Sheppard and many others over many years finally paid off. The Electoral Bill, introducing universal women's suffrage, was passed.

Sheppard received a telegram that read, in part: '[I] trust now that all doubts as to the sincerity of the Government in this very important matter have been effectually removed.' It was signed R. J. Seddon.

It wasn't that Seddon had changed his mind. He had, however, realised that his cause was lost and it would be political suicide to oppose a bill that was going to pass anyway, when it might incur the wrath of 50 per cent of potential voters at the upcoming elections.

Sheppard was under no illusions as to the reasons for his sudden turnaround, but she was more than happy to accept the result. She wrote:

'Now that our political shackles have been removed, a great responsibility is laid on us to use our freedom wisely and well. Let every woman resolve to do so.'

Ettie Rout

Guardian angel of the troops

An Anzac soldier called her 'a second Florence Nightingale'. One newspaper credited her with saving thousands of World War I diggers from death 'or worse'.

But when Ettie Rout died in 1936—by her own hand—she was one of the most despised women in New Zealand.

Rout, who was born in Tasmania in 1877 and grew up in Wellington, had the sort of personality that was always going to polarise people. On one hand she was energetic, intelligent and driven. On the other she spurned convention at a time New Zealand society clung to it—she wore men's clothing, worked for a living (as a court reporter and journalist) and was outspoken on such scandalous issues as sexual equality.

What really got her into trouble—and made her one of New Zealand's greatest women—were her liberal views on contraception and her frank campaign to protect Anzac soldiers from the sexually transmitted diseases that were rampant during World War I.

When war broke out, Rout saw a need for a contingent of mature female volunteers to travel to the fronts and assist medical staff by doing their mundane tasks—cooking, cleaning, bandaging. As was typical with her, she simply went ahead and arranged it, advertising for sound women of good temper to go to Egypt, and appealing for donations to cover their costs.

'We see line upon line of diseased and disabled men filing past for months and maybe for years,' she wrote in an appeal. 'Their call for human help sounds in our ears. Find us unready, they must not.'

Thus Rout's Volunteer Sisterhood was founded. Within months a thousand women had applied, and a few dozen of them began training at Trentham Army camp. The scheme was at first treated with suspicion by the nursing establishment, who feared these untrained women were planning to usurp their positions.

One nurse told the *Poverty Bay Herald* the volunteers were better off staying home and knitting socks: 'It would be madness to send them to Egypt . . . They would simply be in the way. Moreover, they could not stand the climate.'

But go they did, thanks to Rout's tenacity, disdain for conformity, and skill at lobbying authorities and dealing with the media. She eventually got the support of the Minister for Public Health, who dismissed the trained nurses' concerns as 'a misunderstanding', and the first twelve volunteers arrived in Egypt in late 1915.

They, and the women who followed, went on to acquit themselves well, eventually silencing those who'd opposed their mission.

Rout, who arrived in Port Said in February 1916, soon discovered a bigger problem—and one that was to make her even less popular back home.

The troops, she discovered, were riddled with venereal disease, thanks to a combination of battle weariness, boredom, drunkenness and a thriving prostitutes' quarter called the Wazza that was a short distance from their camp.

To the pragmatic Rout, the solution was obvious: hand out condoms and other prophylactics and license brothels that practised safer sex.

'I am quite convinced,' she wrote, 'that whenever society fails to make provision for the normal sexual desires of the average man, endless trouble results.'

Though a few army chiefs were already distributing prophylactics on the quiet, the armed forces and the New Zealand public weren't ready to even acknowledge there was a problem, let alone appear to condone the men's behaviour by issuing condoms.

Rout didn't get very far in her campaign but she did have great success with a more indirect effort. In May 1916 she fundraised for and opened a soldier's club in a little desert town called Tel el Kebir, close to the army camp.

Her idea was to give the soldiers an alternative venue for socialising that didn't put them in the orbit of the prostitutes. It was a wholesome oasis, offering lemon squash, cocoa, cakes, sandwiches, fruit salad and puddings—unheard-of treats for soldiers used to eating bully beef and the equivalent of dog biscuits. And, though the temptations might sound tame compared with those on offer in the Wazza, they worked. The men loved the clubs.

A young Australian soldier wrote to a relative in Christchurch, praising Rout and her tea garden: 'The way she works for the men is great, and I tell you they do appreciate it. She is a second Florence Nightingale . . . One cannot help admiring a woman like that, and she is a thorough lady, too.'

As the men moved on to new battles, Rout would follow them and open a club, often single-handedly. In December 1916, she moved on to England.

Although the clubs had by then proved to be a successful diversion, the problem of sexually transmitted diseases among New Zealand troops throughout Europe and the Middle East was getting worse. In London, Rout noted that thousands of teenage prostitutes lined the Strand. About 20 new cases of venereal disease were reported among New Zealand troops every day.

Rout bailed up the New Zealand High Commissioner to London about the condom issue, as well as top army brass and even visiting New Zealand parliamentarian Sir Joseph Ward, who was deputy leader of the war coalition government. Ward promised to talk to the premier, William Massey.

Though Massey was well aware of the problem, he was constrained by public opinion, which promoted the conservative attitude that venereal disease was a moral problem, not a medical one. Although he asked the British Imperial War Cabinet to clear the streets and camps of prostitutes (the request went unheeded), he assured the New Zealand public that 'the statements that are being made about the prevalence of venereal disease among [the troops] are infamous lies'.

As for distributing condoms, he told the British cabinet: 'I am not prepared as a public man to take the responsibility of doing it. I could not face Parliament with that proposal.'

With the help of a group of English doctors, Rout assembled her own kit of condoms and ointments, and sold it from a soldiers club she set up herself.

Predictably, all hell broke loose back home.

The New Zealand Council of Women passed a resolution at its annual convention expressing its 'bitter abhorrence'—not at the husbands and sons who were playing up—but at 'the affrontery of Ettie Rout in implying that the New Zealand boys must be supplied with remedies to make wrongdoing safe from sin easy. We contend that we send our sons to fight for purity and righteousness and utterly discountenance everything that slackens the moral fibre and self control. We wish to place on record an emphatic repudiation of prophylactics and women who advocate them.'

A deputation of women pounced on Massey, who grumbled that it was a great pity Rout had ever been allowed to leave New Zealand, and promised to have the scheme stopped.

But by then certain key officials had come round to the idea, including New Zealand's surgeon-general—who had the ear of the Minister of Defence, Sir James Allen. Though Massey was still blustering on about Rout, Allen quietly authorised free prophylactic kits for the troops—identical to those Rout had developed—while publicly condemning her. She was never credited, let alone thanked, for developing the kits. In fact the New Zealand Cabinet responded by banning all mention of her from the country's newspapers for the remainder of the war.

With her work done in London, in April 1918 Rout moved to Paris, where she continued to peddle her prophylactic kits. She also pursued the second of the goals in her safer-sex campaign—to tackle the other side of the transaction: the prostitutes.

With the help of local doctor Jean Tissot, she found a comparatively reputable brothel and convinced the owner, a Madame Yvonne, to run it by Rout's rules—weekly medical inspections, impeccable hygiene standards and compulsory prophylactics. In return, Rout would direct New Zealand troops there.

And so she did. She had cards printed for the brothel, with her personal recommendation on the back, and would hand them out at railway stations as troops arrived.

Dr Tissot would later call her 'the real guardian angel of the Anzacs'. But back home her already vocal opponents were incensed. Farcical scenes played out in Parliament: Massey was asked whether his government was aware of Rout's latest disgraceful act but the debate was effectively shut down for fear of exposing women in the public gallery to the sordid details.

One newspaper columnist wrote that the politicians' modesty on the matter was needless 'because nearly all [the ladies] present had read all the stuff beforehand and were present to enjoy the proceedings. In fact, one highly placed lady attended several times on the off chance of it coming before the house.'

The end of the war brought little perspective to the matter in New Zealand. Rout received honours from the British—she was mentioned in dispatches and recognised by the War Office, on behalf of the King, 'for gallant and distinguished services in the field'—and from the French, who gave her their premier decoration for civilian women, the Reconnaissance Française. But in New Zealand she was widely seen as a public enemy, though the RSA secretly sent her a tribute of £100.

One newspaper that stood by her was *New Zealand Truth*. In 1921 it wrote: 'Should Miss Rout return to New Zealand, as *Truth* trusts she may, if only on a brief visit, she will get such a welcome from the workers, their wives, sisters and sweethearts, as well as from the thousands of diggers her strength of mind and unflinching purpose saved from death or worse.'

In fact she returned to New Zealand just once, in 1936, but even then an *Auckland Star* newspaper reporter who spotted her and interviewed her was forbidden by his bosses from writing up the story. She hurriedly announced to her few remaining friends that she had decided to live in the Cook Islands.

Months later she was dead, aged 59, having taken a fatal overdose of quinine. Obituaries ran in several New Zealand newspapers, but none acknowledged the STD prevention work she'd done in the war.

One Australian veteran was outraged that Rout's work wasn't properly acknowledged. He wrote to his country's official war historian: 'It's a fine thing to have the physical courage to go to war for an ideal . . . But it is splendid beyond words to have the moral courage—the fortitude—to do the same thing in the face of being lied about, discredited, slandered and opposed by the very people she was saving—her fellow women safe at home.'

David Low

Courageous cartoonist

Even for a politician, it was a low blow. Neville Chamberlain, Britain's prime minister at the beginning of World War II, told the British Newspaper Society's annual dinner in May 1938 that 'German Nazis have been particularly annoyed by criticisms in the British press and especially by cartoons. The bitter cartoons of Low in the *Evening Standard* have been a frequent source of complaint.'

He didn't mean it as a compliment. In hindsight it's hard to comprehend, but Chamberlain saw New Zealand-born cartoonist David Low as one of his worst enemies in his bid to keep the peace in Europe by building bridges with German leader Adolf Hitler. At that time Britain was following an official policy of appeasement—believing that standing by quietly while Hitler annexed parts of other European countries would fend off another disastrous war.

Low, who'd grown up in Dunedin and Christchurch and had become one of Britain's most famous newspaper cartoonists, was firmly in the other camp. He opposed appeasement and advocated that Britain needed to re-arm, secure the support of the United States and get on side with the Soviet Union. In his cartoons in the *Standard* throughout the 1930s he criticised the British Government and the League of Nations and warned of the combined threats of Hitler, Italian dictator Benito Mussolini and Japan. His views were out of sync even with the newspaper he worked for, whose official editorial line supported Chamberlain's approach.

In July 1936 Low drew a cartoon called 'Stepping stones to glory' showing Hitler blowing raspberries while goose-stepping over the backs of about two dozen men labelled 'spineless leaders of democracy', on the way to a target called 'Boss of the universe'. In February 1938 he warned in a cartoon called 'Increasing Pressure' against British and French complacency. It showed an enormous German soldier leaning heavily on a small man labelled Austria, creating a domino effect that also threatened to collapse figures representing Czechoslovakia, the Balkans, the near East and north-west Europe. At the end of the line, also threatened with being tipped over, a character called Britain says to a character named France: 'Why should we take a stand about someone pushing someone else when it's all so far away?'

'It was very difficult to discuss the Chamberlain policy sensibly in those days,' Low wrote in his 1956 autobiography. 'To his friends he was a saint, to his critics rather less. "He wanted peace"—but so did we all . . . Having committed themselves to a fairytale, [his friends] could not bring themselves to face cold reality. They were determined to wish appeasement into a success.'

The speech by Chamberlain marked the height of Low's battle with the establishment. 'After that,' Low wrote later, 'newspapers that didn't like me referred frequently to my "bad blood cartoons" and my "bitterness". Abuse grew hysterical. "Low is the worst war-monger we have," said a Leftist paper. "Low, politically on the extreme Left, is regarded as the Prime Minister's most powerful enemy," said a right-wing paper . . . People I knew turned away and wouldn't talk to me. Complete strangers held me up in public places and would talk to me. My tobacconist refused to serve me.'

Low did not cower. By then he was used to criticism. He had grown accustomed to getting hate mail and threats from readers. One had called him 'a bloody New Zealand gorilla'. The *Evening Standard* had been banned from Germany in 1933 and Italy in 1935 because of his drawings ridiculing Hitler and Mussolini, and his newspaper's proprietor, Lord Beaverbrook, had warned him not to visit Germany for fear he would meet with an 'accident'. Hitler and his right-hand men repeatedly complained about the 'notorious' cartoonist to the British Foreign Secretary, Lord Halifax. In late 1937 Halifax had put pressure on the chairman of the *Standard*, Michael Wardell, to force Low to tone down his commentary.

Halifax, Wardell and Low had had a meeting, in which Halifax told Low that every one of his critical cartoons was taken at once to the German führer, who would 'blow up'. He described Hitler's propaganda minister Joseph Goebbels 'raging' over a selection of Low's cartoons laid out in a row on a table.

Low later recalled: 'I said something about my having a duty, too, like any other journalist in a democracy whose work had an educative element, to present faithfully the substance of what was happening. I added that although I could understand that the Nazis might find criticism mighty inconvenient, I had difficulty in believing they were so volatile that politeness would cause them to modify their plans.'

However, on that occasion, Low did make a slight compromise. Instead of pillorying Hitler and Mussolini personally, he invented a thinly disguised composite dictator character called Muzzler. A few weeks later Nazi troops invaded Austria. Halifax, as Low saw it, had been taken for a ride, and Low kicked himself for compromising.

He wrote: 'My restraint had been wasted, if indeed I had not by softening protest contributed my mite to a Nazi manoeuvre to weaken Britain morally before this fresh outrage. I considered that [the invasion] let me out and I dropped my politeness.'

Low didn't make the mistake of compromise again. Even after Chamberlain's attack he continued to draw ever more cutting cartoons.

In August 1938 he drew Halifax lying in bed, being asked

by his butler, 'Which backbone shall I lay out this morning, my lord?' Ironically, Hitler was within months referring to Halifax and Chamberlain as 'the spineless worms' over their acquiescence in his annexation of Czechoslovakia. In October Low drew Hitler dressed as a Santa-like figure, throwing into his sack a line of babies named Austria, Czechoslovakia, Poland, Hungary, Yugoslavia, Romania, Bulgaria, Greece and Turkey. The caption read: '"Europe can look forward to a Christmas of peace," says Hitler.'

Though Low had plenty of detractors, he also had supporters. His employer, Lord Beaverbrook, gave him almost free rein, even though the two men were philosophically opposed on key issues. Despite all the hate mail, Beaverbrook believed that Low's cartoons boosted circulation. And the sensitivity of dictators and politicians to his drawings suggests that they feared his influence.

In the wake of perhaps his toughest hours, after Chamberlain's speech, Low received a letter that read: 'A Jewish refugee from Vienna, a very old man personally unknown to you, cannot resist the impulse to tell you how much he admires your glorious art and your inexorable, unfailing criticism.' It was signed Sigmund Freud. (Freud had fled Nazi-occupied Austria for London in June 1938.)

Of course, in September 1939 Low's years of warnings were vindicated when Hitler invaded Poland, and Britain finally declared war on Germany. The following year Chamberlain resigned and was replaced by Winston Churchill, whom Low admired, though not without reservation, and had a reasonably friendly relationship with.

(Churchill had cheekily written in 1932 that Low was a 'particularly mischievous' green-eyed Antipodean radical: 'Low's pencil is not only servile. It is essentially mutinous. You cannot bridle the wild ass of the desert, still less prohibit its natural hee-haw.')

Throughout the war Low fought on against Hitler with his pen.

Though by now he was in step with Britain's leaders and the general public—or, more accurately, Britain had fallen into step with his views, the personal danger to him had not passed. Shortly after the Allied withdrawal from Dunkirk in mid-1940, Low learned he was high up on a Gestapo hit list. Should Germany invade Britain—which at that point was a distinct possibility—he was unlikely to survive. He quickly made arrangements to secure a bolt-hole outside London and new identities for his mother, aunt, wife and two daughters, should an invasion happen. As for his own safety, he refused an offer of safe passage to Canada, made the token effort of shaving off his beard, and continued drawing Hitler and his cronies with even more vehemence.

'I decided to stay put, partly because I had intense curiosity to see what would happen and partly because I knew two trusted friends who were cherishing an old printing-press which might conceivably do for an underground paper.'

Of course he didn't get a chance to realise his ambition of launching a Resistance communications network, but neither did he pull any punches. Though he largely stepped in behind Churchill, he railed against the hypocrisies of those people who were on the one hand nobly riding out the war in an atmosphere of communal co-operation, and on the other cheating on their food rations, thieving, exploiting others in need and taking advantage of positions of power ('little Hitlers exceeding their brief authority', he called them). He also criticised the government for indiscriminately locking up foreigners, whether foe or friend, including a friend of his who was a Czech artist.

Low—and Britain—survived the war. He was knighted in 1962, having refused the honour in the 1930s, and died in London in 1963, aged 72.

A former *Evening Standard* editor and British MP, Michael Foot, said that though Low's voice wasn't a lone one in the late 1930s, his 'was amongst the first and the bravest and the most effective and persistent'.

'He never wavered wherever the threat appeared,' said Foot in 1985. 'David Low saw the reality here as elsewhere, and nothing could stop him showing it . . . No tribute is too strong to express what liberals and democrats owed to him in the age of Hitler and Mussolini, of Chamberlain and Halifax.'

Low's biographers, Colin Seymour-Ure and Jim Schoff, said he provoked strong reactions in huge audiences and was palpably in touch with them. 'Talk of [his] impact in the abrupt manner of an earthquake is too crude. Low's influence, surely, was more atmospheric, part of the air people breathed.'

Sir Edmund Hillary

Hero of the Sherpas

Two fateful moments determined Edmund Hillary's path in life. One was when his mate George Lowe suggested he join an expedition to the Himalayas. The other came on an icy evening several years later when he sat down to a smoky campfire in a barren and windy hollow beside a Himalayan glacier.

The consequences of the first moment are well known. On 29 May 1953 Hillary become the first man to step on to the summit of Mt Everest. The bewildered 33-year-old Tuakau beekeeper was immediately knighted and propelled into instant international stardom, forever to be known as the conqueror of Everest.

The latter was a far quieter moment, but one that put Hillary on a path that he came to regard as far more worthwhile and satisfying. More than even his pioneering climb, it marked him as a hero.

It was October 1960 and Hillary was on a yeti-hunting expedition in the Himalayas. It was by no means a pleasant spot to camp—4900 metres above sea level and beside the formidable Tolam Bau glacier—but Hillary hardly noticed. He quickly became engrossed in a conversation with his expedition members and Sherpa companions that would last several hours. He didn't find a yeti on that trip, but he did find a project that would consume him for his remaining 47 years.

Even as the fire sank lower and the cold tightened its grip on the shivering gathering, the dozen men talked as energetically as if they'd been in a cosy pub.

This is how Hillary remembered it:

'Urkien [Sherpa] took a handful of stunted azalea and threw it on the fire. It flared up with a crackle of sparks and threw into relief the bearded, restless faces of the sahibs and the strong, poised countenances of the Sherpas against the desolate background of our campsite.

'In a warm flood of memory I dwelt on the many things we had gained over the years from our Sherpas. Not only help in the physical sense—so many loads carried here, so many risks taken there, or so many lives (alas) lost somewhere else. But few of us had failed to learn something from the character and temperament of the men themselves—their hardiness and cheerfulness, their vigour and loyalty, and their freedom from our civilised curse of self-pity.'

Hillary turned to Urkien, the tempestuous but tough Sherpa leader on that expedition. The New Zealander had long enjoyed his good-humoured company and respected his intelligence. 'Tell us, Urkien, if there were one thing we could do for your village, what should it be?'

His friend replied: 'We would like our children to go to school, sahib. Of all the things you have, learning is the one we most desire for our children. With all respect, sahib, we know you have little to teach us in strength and toughness. We do not envy you your restless spirits—perhaps we are happier and more content than you are? But knowledge for our children—that we would like to see.'

Hillary, who'd been raised with strong values of social responsibility, didn't need to be convinced. Later, he explained: 'You'd have to be a clot not to realise the problems faced by people like the Sherpas . . . They had done so much for me and had so little. My family training simply swung into place. Instead of just idly talking about the Sherpas' problems, I decided I should jolly well do something about them.'

'Together,' he told Urkien, 'we will build a school.'

It wasn't the easiest of building projects. The first hurdle was money. Though they secured a donated prefabricated aluminium building from a company in neighbouring India, and the Sherpas of the village were happy to contribute their labour, they were going to need about $US9000, mostly to cover transport costs. As he would do many times in the next half century, Hillary went cap in hand on behalf of the people of Nepal.

This is where his legendary modesty and selflessness paid off. In 1959 he had applied to a United States encyclopaedia publisher, Field Enterprises, for funding for the yeti-hunting expedition, which was to double as a scientific study into the effects of high altitude on the body. The company had flown him to Chicago to discuss it.

One of the executives later recalled the meeting: 'Here was this guy Hillary who'd climbed Everest and got a knighthood for it, the lot. We didn't know Ed too well at that stage–he was a nice guy, sure, but we knew he wouldn't be working with an outfit like us for nothing. Probably, he'd have a bunch of lawyers and accountants with him–but we reckoned we could handle them.

'Then in comes this tall guy, by himself, with his hair all over the place and carrying an old briefcase held together with string. Well, that threw us right from the start. And then when we came to the bit where we asked how much he would like for himself, he says, "Well, on an expedition we don't usually take any money for ourselves."

'We didn't know whether he meant it. For a bit we thought he might just be the coolest cat we'd ever met. Then we began to feel sorry for him. We felt we had to help this guy–force him to take the money. Up till then I'd never been able to understand why he hadn't made a million bucks out of Everest. I think Ed's the most honest guy I've ever met–I'm not sure he's not the only honest guy I've ever met.'

So when Hillary got in touch again the following year to ask for a relatively modest donation for the school the company readily consented, confident that the New Zealander would not squander their money. (They also bought him a new briefcase.)

The next problem Hillary and the Sherpas faced was logistical. They had settled on a site for the school in Khumjung, a village 4000 metres above sea level that clings to the side of the mountain Khumbila, a close neighbour of Everest. It was more than 270 steep kilometres from the nearest city, Kathmandu, and there were no roads. It had earlier taken Hillary nine days to walk the route, unencumbered and walking vigorously. It was too much to ask the Sherpa porters to carry in the building materials on their backs—some of the aluminium sheets were three metres long.

A solution soon presented itself. A few months later a pilot for the Red Cross approached Hillary. He needed somewhere to drop relief packages to Tibetan refugees fleeing Chinese rule in their homeland. Did Hillary know a good spot?

In fact, Hillary had already discovered a suitable, if somewhat precarious, site in the Mingbo Valley, which was still a day's walk from Khumjung. They made a deal—Hillary would level and clear the land for a landing strip and the pilot would fly in the aluminium sheets for the school, as well as the relief packages.

Creating the airstrip had its own challenges, not least of which were the large boulders that marked the site, some two metres high and weighing several tonnes. Without hope of getting heavy equipment to the site and with no explosives, they would have to be removed by hand.

Hillary later recalled, with characteristic understatement: 'The boulders were singularly unresponsive to the blows of our sledgehammer.' Hillary's team of Sherpas came up with a solution: they dug enormous craters next to each boulder and levered the rocks in.

It wasn't the most forgiving of airstrips, and was condemned by horrified aviation authorities several months later, but the pilot was as good as his word. By the time the airfield was closed there was a pile of aluminium sheets in the village.

'For six days,' Hillary later recalled, 'we worked like madmen on the job—putting in rock foundations and wooden floors; assembling walls and trusses; attaching the roof sheets; fitting doors and windows; and bolting and screwing the whole thing down to the foundations. Our task was made more difficult by our inability to follow the assembly instructions. We were rather shaken, late one evening, to complete the roof and find we had three sheets of corrugated aluminium left over.'

Still, Hillary's two-classroom schoolhouse in the clouds was opened in June 1961 with 45 pupils, less than a year after that fateful campfire conversation—and still stands today, now part of a complex that accommodates more than 350 children, from pre-schoolers to teenagers.

Hillary left for home shortly after the opening ceremony. 'I little realised I was leaving behind what was to become a new way of life for me.'

He simply couldn't stop there. Requests started trickling in from other Himalayan communities. One letter read: 'We the local people, the Sherpas of Thami, Khumbu, came to know that your honour, helping us in all respects, is going to open some more schools in Khumbu. So we Thami people are requesting your honour to open a school at Thami just like Khumjung. Though our children have eyes but still they are blind! So all we Sherpas of Thami are praying your honour to make our children just like those in Khumjung. We hope your honour may consider our prayer.'

So Hillary went from conqueror of Everest to builder of schools. Field Enterprises stayed on as a sponsor and in return Hillary gave up a year of his life to tour the United States delivering lectures under the publishing company's banner.

While there he struck a deal with the Sears Roebuck shopping chain to be an advisor on camping equipment, and also became a director for a Field Enterprises Australian subsidiary. He took a modest income from these ventures, and from writing several books, to support his wife Louise and their three children, but he was never the wealthy man he could have been. Instead he devoted much of his time and money to raising more money for development projects and travelling to the Himalayas to oversee them—while having a few mountaineering adventures along the way.

Hillary and his Himalayan Trust went on to build more than 25 schools in the following half century. They came to be known as the Hillary Schools. It was a great gift for the people who'd helped him reach the top of Everest.

Hillary and the trust, working with locals and volunteers from around the world, also tackled other needs within the Sherpa community—building bridges and another airstrip, installing water pipelines, repairing monasteries, improving health care, building hospitals and protecting the environment. Hillary was the public face of the trust and travelled the world raising money for it, with the help of his equally dedicated wife. They were careful not to waste any of the precious money on their own expenses, instead privately funding their own trips to the Himalayas. Louise also wrote books to supplement the family's income.

Hillary's impact on the Sherpa community could hardly be understated. In 1963 he was in the Himalayas with an expedition team when smallpox broke out. He and the team immediately arranged a massive programme of vaccinations. At least 25 people died but the 7000 vaccinations undoubtedly averted a disaster.

'You have saved all our lives,' the leaders of Khumjung village told Hillary and his men. 'But for you we would all now be dead.'

Hillary's dedication came at an enormous personal cost. On 31

March 1975 Louise and their youngest child, Belinda, were planning to fly in from Kathmandu to join Hillary as he built a major hospital in the village of Phaphlu. The plane crashed on take-off. Louise and Belinda were killed instantly.

Hillary's world caved in. But even in the darkest moment of his life he stayed true to his mission. Five days after the tragedy he wrote a letter to friends and family in New Zealand. 'God knows if I'll have the courage to go on living,' he wrote. But, he said, he intended to restart work on the hospital within days. 'Whatever happens I feel the task must be finished.'

Even as they mourned, the heartbroken Hillary family–Ed, his elder children Peter and Sarah and his brother Rex–returned to Phaphlu. Though they endured a great emotional struggle, the hospital was completed in December that year.

Despite ongoing problems with altitude sickness, Hillary continued his work in the Himalayas until his death in 2007, at the age of 88.

American author Cynthia Russ Ramsay wrote in her book *Sir Edmund Hillary and the People of Everest* that Hillary's commitment never wavered. She dubbed his development campaign a one-man foreign-aid programme:

'An earnest and deeply felt sense of justice and duty transformed Hillary, the conqueror of Everest, the somewhat reckless athlete, into a father figure and humanitarian. With the Khumjung School . . . a new way of life was beginning for the Sherpas. For Hillary, with such exploits as scaling peaks and trekking across Antarctica long behind him, a greater adventure had begun.'

In the foreword to Russ Ramsay's book, Prince Philip said Hillary's life was inspired and directed by his devotion to the Sherpa people. 'It would be difficult to exaggerate the value of his thoughtful and sensitive contribution to their welfare and to the conservation of their way of life in the spectacular Himalayan environment.'

Hillary once said that the Everest climb had enabled him to lead exactly the kind of life he'd always wanted to. 'The trouble with Everest,' he said, 'is that so many people look upon it as the peak for me. The implication is that after Everest everything I do is on the decline. That's just not true. My life didn't end with Everest. It began.'

Justice Peter Mahon

Upholder of justice

Captain Jim Collins had a spring in his step as he walked through Auckland International Airport early on the morning of 28 November 1979. The 45-year-old pilot was looking forward to taking command of TE901, Air New Zealand's 14th non-stop sightseeing flight over Antarctica, with co-pilot Gregory Cassin by his side. Both men were experienced and highly regarded pilots. Neither had flown the route before.

The cabin of the DC-10 aircraft buzzed with anticipation, as the 237 passengers enjoyed a champagne breakfast and chatted with explorer and mountaineer Peter Mulgrew. Passengers were encouraged to move around the cabin, sharing occupancy of the coveted window seats to snap photographs of the vast wilderness below.

When they reached the pack ice, four hours into the 8000-kilometre return journey, Mulgrew moved up to the jump seat to conduct a live commentary over the PA system. As they approached Ross Island, the landscape was covered in cloud. Collins obtained clearance from MAC Center, US air traffic control at McMurdo Station, to descend in a figure of eight through a gap in the clouds, from 16,000 feet to 2000 feet. They would fly below the cloud cover to allow passengers a better view—it was after all, a scenic flight.

After levelling out at 1500 feet, Collins returned to the computer navigation system, which was locked on a pre-programmed course

Kate Sheppard fought quietly but doggedly for women's rights in New Zealand. Thanks in large part to her efforts, in 1893 New Zealand women were the first in the world to be granted universal suffrage.

Ettie Rout defied the conventions of conservative New Zealand society to hand out condoms to World War I soldiers. She was later credited with saving countless lives, but committed suicide in 1936, depressed and alone.

Cartoonist David Low made it onto the Gestapo most-wanted list for his warnings in British papers in the 1930s of the threat of Hitler and Mussolini. His campaign was vindicated when World War II began in 1939. Low (*right*) is shown here with journalist Gerry Harcourt-Wybert in London in 1957.

Sir Edmund Hillary (pictured with fellow Mt Everest climber Tenzing Norgay) devoted most of his life to quietly and determinedly improving the education and health of the Sherpa people of Nepal.

Prime Minister David Lange's election night celebrations in 1984 were overshadowed by threats from the United States and Australia to cast New Zealand out of ANZUS should Lange go ahead with his party's plan to declare the country nuclear free.

Member of Parliament Marilyn Waring (pictured with former National Prime Minister Keith Holyoake) crossed the floor in 1984 hoping to force her domineering leader, Sir Robert Muldoon, to call a snap election on the nuclear issue. It worked.

TE WHITI.

Maori spiritual leader and pacifist Te Whiti o Rongomai lead an inspirational campaign of peaceful resistance against the colonial New Zealand government in the late nineteenth century.

Garfield Todd was a Protestant missionary to Southern Rhodesia (now Zimbabwe) who became the country's prime minister. He introduced revolutionary reforms to redress the imbalance between whites and blacks in the country and later become an outspoken opponent of white rule.

Dame Whina Cooper was a widely admired Maori leader who led a historic hikoi the length of the North Island in 1975 to protest against the loss of Maori land. She is pictured here with Minister of Maori Affairs, Duncan McIntyre in 1976.

he believed would take them straight up McMurdo Sound to Scott Base. Visual landmarks were noted to the left and right, considered to be the headlands at the entrance to the sound.

Up ahead they could see only a flat expanse of snow stretching 50 or 60 kilometres beneath the cloud. But if this was the Ross Ice Shelf, where were the buildings and radio aerials of the MAC Center?

'I don't like this,' said flight engineer officer Gordon Brook.

Collins decided to pull away. Twenty seconds passed.

'Whoop whoop. Pull up. Whoop whoop.'

Ground clearance was dropping, 500 feet . . . 400 feet.

'Whoop Whoop.'

'Go round power please,' said Collins in a firm, steady voice.

'Whoop whoop. Pull . . .'

It was an ordinary day in the number one courtroom of the Auckland Supreme Court. Justice Peter Mahon spent the morning of 28 November 1979 listening to plaintiff and defence counsel tussle over damages for injury in a motor vehicle accident. In his eight years at the bench he'd presided over many such cases, necessary but at times tedious work for one of the country's pre-eminent judges.

Driving home that evening, he listened to a radio report about an Air New Zealand aircraft missing over Antarctica. By the following morning the worst had been confirmed; just after 12.49 p.m. New Zealand time, Flight TE901 had slammed straight into the northern slopes of Mt Erebus, killing all aboard. The aircraft disintegrated on impact, the wreckage strewn in a great black smudge across the snow.

As Mahon pored over the *New Zealand Herald*, questions were already being asked. Mt Erebus was 3794 metres high and the plane was flying in broad daylight, with clear air and good weather. The aircraft was equipped with the most-sophisticated computer navigation system available. How could this happen?

Four months later the New Zealand government would appoint Mahon as a one-man Royal Commission of Inquiry tasked with answering that very question. Mahon, 56, was highly regarded within the legal profession. As a barrister and crown solicitor he had been a formidable advocate; as a judge he was eloquent and incisive. He was also a gifted writer.

Leading the site investigation for Operation Overdue was chief air accident inspector Ron Chippindale. For the former air force pilot and his team, it was a gruelling task hampered by poor weather. Within days the cockpit voice recorder and digital flight data recorder were recovered, along with the cockpit flight panel and more than 200 cameras. The mystery of flight TE901 continued to deepen; there had been no equipment malfunction, no emergency calls and the cockpit voice recordings revealed no concerns until just seconds before impact.

Chippindale's report was published by the New Zealand government—against the wishes of Mahon and Air New Zealand—in June 1980, just days before the Royal Commission of Inquiry was due to begin. Chippindale concluded that pilot error was the 'probable cause' of the accident—Captain Collins had made a fundamental mistake in descending below the limit of 16,000 feet specified by Civil Aviation and Air New Zealand, and in remaining low while uncertain of their position.

The finding of pilot error made headlines around the world. A map published with the report showing the plane's figure-of-eight descent led to a widespread perception that the plane had been lost, flying hopelessly in circles through the clouds. In fact, photographs taken by passengers just moments before impact showed that the plane was flying in clear air.

When the inquiry into the cause of the crash opened on 7 July 1980, it was widely anticipated that the eventual report would endorse Chippindale's findings. Mahon later wrote that he had also expected this would be the 'probable sequel'. But first there were two fundamental questions to be answered: why was the plane flying at 1500 feet, when Air New Zealand claimed there was a rigidly maintained minimum safe altitude of 16,000 feet? And why was it flying at this height on a course that led it directly into the side of Mt Erebus?

Finding the answers would take 75 days, 3083 pages of evidence, 284 documentary exhibits and 368 pages of closing submissions. Witness after witness for Air New Zealand, including chief executive Morrie Davis, denied knowledge of the practice of low flying, but it soon became clear that most of the previous scenic flights had flown as low as 2000 feet over McMurdo Sound to give passengers a better view. This information had appeared in journalists' reports of the scenic flights and in photographs used in Air New Zealand's own publicity material.

Furthermore, at a briefing several days before the flight, Collins and Cassin had been shown the coordinates to be programmed into the aircraft's computer navigation system. These would take the flight directly over McMurdo Sound, where Collins and Cassin were advised that in clear conditions they could descend lower than 6000 feet at the invitation of the controllers at MAC Center.

The night before the flight, Collins used these coordinates to plot the route over McMurdo Sound on a topographical map. Unbeknown to Collins and the crew, eight hours before take-off the coordinates of the last leg of the flight path were altered by Air New Zealand's navigation section, shifting the destination waypoint 43 kilometres to the east. If this part of the route was flown at an altitude below 13,000 feet, the aircraft was programmed to fly directly into Mt Erebus.

Crucial evidence was also given by Captain Gordon Vette, who produced a paper outlining his research into the polar ocular illusion known as 'sector whiteout', where solid cloud cover and unrelenting snow meet, creating the appearance of flat terrain and a distant horizon. In the absence of any landmarks, it was almost impossible for the crew to see that the snowscape was in fact rising to meet the clouds at an angle of 15 degrees. Even seconds before impact the crew would not have been able to see the mountain.

When the report of the inquiry was finally released on 27 April 1981, it revealed that Mahon rejected Chippindale's findings of pilot error. He exonerated the crew and found that the single dominant cause of the accident lay in the airline's alteration of the flight path coordinates without telling the crew. It was the crew's mistaken belief that they were flying over McMurdo Sound, combined with the whiteout illusion, that caused the plane to fly straight into the side of Mt Erebus.

But it was Mahon's conclusion on the evidence presented by Air New Zealand that was most damning.

'No judicial officer ever wishes to be compelled to say that he has listened to evidence which is false. He always prefers to say, as I hope the hundreds of judgments which I have written will illustrate, that he cannot accept the relevant explanation, or that he prefers a contrary version of events.

'But in this case, the palpably false sections of evidence I heard could not have been the result of mistake, or faulty recollection. They originated, I am compelled to say, in a pre-determined plan of deception. They were very clearly part of an attempt to conceal a series of disastrous administrative blunders, and so . . . I am forced, reluctantly, to say that I had to listen to an orchestrated litany of lies.'

Mahon ordered the airline to pay the costs incurred by the representatives of the passengers, the New Zealand Airline Pilots Association, and the estates of the pilot and co-pilot. He also ordered the airline to pay $150,000 towards the government's costs.

The night before the report was to be delivered to parliament and released to the media, Mahon spent time with his son Sam, which Sam recalled in his book *In My Father's Shadow: A Portrait of Justice Peter Mahon.* 'Peter standing with his gun broken over his arm, with the characteristic cigarette, staring out across the grey unbroken waters, surrounded by the leafless willows and waiting for gunfire. "Tomorrow, all hell's going to break loose." . . . I glanced at him and I remember his face turned to the hills with his eyes set on that bright line where the sun had just gone down.'

Break loose it did. The findings were a disaster for the state-owned airline and its executives, further undermining public confidence and opening the door to compensation claims. Mahon was publicly savaged by Prime Minister Rob Muldoon, who refused to accept the report. Davis–a friend of Muldoon's–retired, and politicians, pilots and commentators weighed in from all sides.

Air New Zealand immediately sought a judicial review of Mahon's findings of conspiracy. The Court of Appeal upheld the claim, ruling Mahon did not have the jurisdiction to make a finding of conspiracy and, even if he had the authority, he breached 'the most basic principles of natural justice' by not allowing the airline an opportunity to refute the allegations of conspiracy. The order for punitive costs against Air New Zealand was reversed.

A shocked Mahon resigned, stating that the minority judgment of Justices Woodhouse and McMullin implied he was incompetent as a judge and made his position untenable. Mahon asked the government to appeal to the Privy Council on behalf of the Royal Commission, on the grounds that the court had misconceived the role of a Royal Commission and that both Woodhouse and McMullin had children who worked for Air New Zealand creating questions over the propriety of their adjudicating on the matter. The Privy Council paid tribute to Mahon's 'brilliant and painstaking investigative work' but found there was no probative evidence to support his finding of conspiracy and upheld the Court of Appeal's ruling.

Supporters of Air New Zealand claimed the airline was vindicated by the decisions of the Court of Appeal and Privy Council. In fact, Mahon's findings as to the causes of the crash were never challenged.

After his resignation Mahon found himself shunned by many of his former colleagues. An application for a lecturing position at Canterbury University received no reply and, without a judicial pension, he took up a practising certificate so that he could give legal opinions, a move criticised by some in the profession as going against convention.

He wrote a bestselling book, *Verdict on Erebus*, giving his account of the inquiry; the book won the 1985 New Zealand Book Award for non-fiction. He later took up a part-time lecturing position at Auckland University.

In 1984, 48 eminent New Zealanders, including Sian Elias (who later become the country's chief justice), Anand Satyanand (later governor-general), academics and politicians, petitioned the newly elected Prime Minister David Lange to nominate Mahon for a knighthood. The petition was rejected.

Mahon died in 1986 at the age of 62.

On 25 August 1999, Maria Collins, Ann Cassin and Margarita Mahon—the widows of Jim Collins, Gregory Cassin and Peter Mahon—sat in the House of Parliament as transport minister Maurice Williamson finally tabled the report of the commission of inquiry, giving it official status 18 years after it was delivered. Williamson called Mahon 'one of New Zealand's true heroes'.

'The International Civil Aviation Organization states that Mahon's report was ten years ahead of its time, and I believe that to be true.' said Williamson. 'The International Civil Aviation Organization goes even further and states that subsequent high-technology systems catastrophes, such as those of Chernobyl and Bhopal, need not have happened if the international safety community had grasped the messages from the Erebus report and adopted those preventative lessons.

'Justice Mahon's report richly deserves this House's recognition. Erebus was an awful tragedy, but it would be unconscionable if we ignored the lessons that Justice Mahon so clearly enunciated.'

Gordon Vette resigned from Air New Zealand after the inquiry. He was later granted an honorary doctorate from Glasgow University, and in 2007 was appointed an Officer of the New Zealand Order of Merit for services to aviation. Vette's findings on systemic deficiencies contributing to the Erebus crash is widely recognised as changing the approach to crash investigations worldwide. The Airline Pilots Association awarded the Jim Collins Memorial Award for exceptional contributions to air safety to both Vette (1991) and Mahon (posthumously in 2009).

In November 2009, the 30th anniversary of the crash, Air New Zealand chief executive Rob Fyfe apologised to those affected by the tragedy for Air New Zealand's failures and its treatment of the victims' families.

Sam Mahon told the *New Zealand Herald*, 'My father was one of the bravest men I have known. We didn't agree on a lot of things but . . . he would never run away from a fight. So they picked the wrong man to try to squeeze.

For any of us to be able to stand up, and say "these people should be held to account" is great. Because in this country . . . nobody ever takes account for their actions.'

Phillida Bunkle
Sandra Coney
Clare Matheson

Standing up for the powerless

It was 1975 and Phillida Bunkle was almost nine months pregnant with her first child. She turned up for her last antenatal appointment and the doctor began his examination.

'[He] suddenly grunted and using all his strength pushed his finger through my cervix. "That'll get you going, my girl," he said, and indeed it did. I started to bleed and was admitted to the hospital during the night.'

The doctor arrived: 'Who's a silly girl then?' he asked Bunkle, then in her early thirties.

'I'm not a silly girl,' she replied. 'I'm a woman and I'm frightened, and I want to know what's going on.'

It was a bad start to what would turn into a traumatic experience. The baby wasn't ready to be born but could no longer stay in the womb, so intervention after intervention followed to coerce and force the child out.

'As the doctor bullied and yelled and threatened,' she later wrote, 'it became apparent that this was his theatre and his drama . . . The message was clear: I was a germ-filled impediment to the successful delivery of his baby. I was a naughty girl for defying his expertise, but I would get off more lightly if I didn't make a fuss.

'Finally it came to an end–picking up the scissors, he took three scrunches into my vagina, wrenched the forceps, removed the baby and slowly, very slowly, started stitching. As the needle stabbed and the thread sawed, I watched his face, alive with pleasure. It grew with each stab as he punched out his frustrations at the preceding hours.'

He had an anaesthetic at the ready but he didn't use it. 'It was my first experience of total powerlessness,' said Bunkle. 'I had simply assumed there were laws against this sort of thing.'

Sandra Coney had a similar experience, as did many women in that era. She was just eighteen when she had her first child. Staff refused to call her husband so she laboured alone. Through the walls of her room she could hear nurses scolding other labouring women for being noisy. At one point she was used as a model to demonstrate breast binding to the staff–and they didn't ask first.

'It was not that giving birth had been physically difficult, but that I had never before felt so helpless, so at the mercy of people whom I could not trust,' she later wrote.

But the indignities of their run-ins with the health service are eclipsed by the story they would soon hear from Clare Matheson.

In June 1964, at the age of 27, Matheson had a miscarriage. Weeks later the mother of two was bleeding and was concerned that it could be symptomatic of cancer. She went to her GP for a smear test. A few days later she got a phone call from her GP's nurse to say she had an appointment at National Women's Hospital, in the Auckland suburb of Greenlane.

'What's the appointment for?' Matheson asked.

'I don't know,' was the reply. 'They'll tell you when you get there.'

In August, two months after the miscarriage, Matheson reported to the reception desk at the hospital's gynaecological clinic. After a wait, she was ushered in to see an intern.

'A battery of personal questions was fired at me, delivered with military precision and an expression of complete boredom and lack of interest,' she recalled in her 1989 memoir *Fate Cries Enough*.

She was then directed to a small cubicle and asked to lie down on a hard bed, half naked.

'The smell of hospital, the clink of kidney trays and the deep mutterings of expertise were all around me . . . I felt vulnerable and nervous. I had yet to meet one smiling face, or hear one encouraging or supportive word.'

In walked a tall, solid man of about 50 with a long face and heavy jaw. It was Herbert Green, associate professor of obstetrics and gynaecology at the University of Auckland Medical School. He examined her and asked about her symptoms in a pleasant, if superior, manner. He told her a few cells were not normal but he didn't think it was anything to worry about.

'A close watch would be kept on my condition and he recommended I have a biopsy under anaesthetic within a few months . . . He was very casual about everything and obviously not in the least bit worried about my condition. His confidence was reassuring.'

Matheson was relieved. It didn't sound as if she had cancer.

When she turned up for the biopsy, the professor had changed his mind about it. He told her it wasn't necessary. 'He explained that he and others once believed that abnormal cells led to cancer and that hysterectomies used to be carried out on women with my condition. Lots of women, he said, had had hysterectomies needlessly.'

He assured Matheson that she would be kept under observation and should have regular check-ups at the clinic.

She did have a colposcopy on that visit, in which the cervix is examined for abnormalities with a magnifying instrument. The presiding doctor was a younger clinician called Bill McIndoe. 'He was very courteous,' she recalled, 'and did everything possible to make an embarrassing examination as bearable as possible.'

She was discharged immediately afterwards believing nothing was amiss. After many weeks of worry, relief flooded through her.

'I was delighted with the outcome and most impressed . . . I was a complete optimist and trusted people implicitly. I had great admiration for those who had succeeded academically, and doctors, of course, were placed high in this category.'

On her next visit to her GP, she asked the nurse why she hadn't been told about the suspicious smear test. 'She replied that some women got so upset by such information and made such a fuss, that it was better not to tell them.'

In fact, there was a less benevolent factor in play. Green didn't believe the prevailing view among the medical profession that a lesion on the cervix called carcinoma-in-situ (CIS) was a precursor of invasive cervical cancer, and he had set out to prove his theory, using the women who attended his hospital as study material.

He had decided to treat conservatively a selection of his patients who had been diagnosed with CIS. By 1967 they numbered 27. He would let their conditions advance naturally, while monitoring them. He wrote in a medical journal that as long as a cervix appeared normal there was no 'therapeutic emergency' or risk to the patient. 'By avoiding alarm and arranging admission to suit the patient, her co-operation is retained far more easily.'

The women were kept in the dark not only about the study, but also about their medical conditions. Matheson's smear test had showed that the abnormalities in the cells of her cervix were suggestive of malignancy. Such tests were graded on a scale of one to five; one being normal, five being conclusively malignant. Matheson had scored a three. Without her knowledge, let alone her consent, Green decided to add her to his study. He would monitor her condition, but not treat it.

In the 15 years that followed, Matheson went to the hospital 44 times. She endured internal examinations, colposcopies, smear tests and biopsies. On six occasions she was put under a general anaesthetic and operated on. Believing she was in good health, she came to regard the visits as little more than tiresome and intrusive inconveniences.

'The whole business was humiliating and embarrassing. Lining up as in a cattle race, impersonal faces giving directions, moving here, moving there at somebody's whim, having to strip off half my clothes, personal questions, personal examinations, and little apparent humanity anywhere.'

What she didn't know was that in late 1967 her smear tests had begun to score fives. In her patient files (which she wasn't shown) the doctors wrote: 'Cells conclusive for malignancy.' By late 1969 she was diagnosed with CIS. In the early 1970s the word 'tumour' began to appear in her files. She remained oblivious.

The doctors could see the abnormalities growing in her cervix but most of the time took only enough tissue in each biopsy for analysis—for the sake of the study they were careful not to remove all the lesions.

Meanwhile, Green continued to report to the medical journals. In 1970 he wrote in the *Australian and New Zealand Journal of Obstetrics and Gynaecology*: 'The only way to settle finally the problem of what happens to in-situ cancer is to follow indefinitely patients with diagnosed but untreated lesions. This is being attempted.'

In the August 1969 issue of the *International Journal of Obstetrics and Gynaecology*, he wrote: 'If the physician does not worry too much about the disease, then neither will the patient!'

By 1974 Matheson had been visiting Green's clinic for ten years and was confident she was in sound health. She had three children and was studying history at Auckland University so the visits were becoming even more inconvenient.

'After all the years of going in and out of hospital,' she wrote later, 'I really could not see the point of it all. I felt I had been going in there long enough. As I had been assured that there was no cause to worry about cancer, the wild thought came to me that perhaps there was some other purpose behind it all. What, I could not imagine, but the whole business made no sense to me.'

When she next saw Green she made a comment that 'intimated that perhaps I was being used as a guinea pig, and that they could find someone else'.

'His reaction seemed far more violent than my comment had warranted. "You'll do as you're told," he said loudly, his face flushed with anger. It is difficult to respond to that kind of comment when one is flat on one's back and half clothed. I lay there feeling like a chastised child. So I continued to do as I was told.'

Green's outburst might have been symptomatic of pressures that he was coming under in the hospital. Dr McIndoe and his colleague Dr Jock McLean had begun to complain about Green to the hospital hierarchy, alarmed by the number of women developing cancer. They were gutsy to speak out about a senior colleague in an environment that evidently valued loyalty above transparency but their concerns were repeatedly dismissed.

Professor Denis Bonham, then Green's head of department, was later quoted as believing the struggle between Green and McIndoe was no more than a clash of personalities. McIndoe, he said, was charming but had a vicious streak. Green was a 'free thinker'. 'No one would be unhappy with the way he managed the patients with cancer. He really looked after them fantastically.'

In the late 1970s, Matheson's smear tests unexpectedly returned to normal. Though the pathology from an examination in 1977 had shown abnormalities that might have pointed to invasive cancer,

Green dismissed it as 'somewhat surprising', and discharged her in 1979.

He wrote to her GP: 'I do not think she needs to attend clinic for further follow-up as she has no more chance than the next person of now developing any carcinoma of the cervix.'

Her case appeared, to Green at least, to have backed up his theory. Though it was still in evidence, the CIS hadn't led to invasive cancer. Or so he let himself believe.

Matheson and her family were delighted when she was discharged after so many years. 'We believed that Professor Green had monitored my condition and that I had never approached any condition that looked like cancer.'

But in 1985 Matheson, by then the deputy principal of Kelston Girls' High School in west Auckland, had another abnormal smear—a grade three. Green had retired so her GP gave her an unsealed letter referring her to another gynaecologist. She opened it. For the first time she learned that she'd had CIS. She didn't even know what it was.

'I got out my nursing daughter's medical dictionary and looked up the term. "A condition which left untreated can lead to truly invasive cancer." I shook with emotion. I was deeply shocked, furious that I had never been told this, and now also fearful about what my present condition might be . . . What right had they to keep me in ignorance of my own condition?'

The new gynaecologist obtained her records from National Women's Hospital. He told her he would have performed a hysterectomy 15 years earlier. 'You were left sitting on a time-bomb,' he said. For the first time Matheson found out about the grade five smears. She had another biopsy. It confirmed she had invasive cervical cancer.

Almost immediately, the new gynaecologist arranged for Matheson to have treatment with radioactive rods followed by a radical hysterectomy, which immediately brought on menopause. Her fight against cancer was won. Her fight against the health system was just beginning.

'The thought of the professor messing around with my anatomy for so long, until it was virtually unrecognisable, for goodness knows what reason, made me feel used. I could only liken it to how I thought a woman would feel after being raped. Something forced upon her, without her consent. By why? Despite the feeling I had of being emotionally battered, I was determined that I would not submit passively to the situation.'

Still unsuspecting of Green's wider agenda, she turned first to her GP, whom she discovered had been sending annual reports to National Women's since her discharge saying she was 'alive and well with no evidence of cancer'. But the GP had not carried out any tests in that time, or physically examined her.

She took the GP to the Medical Practitioners' Disciplinary Committee, which reprimanded him and fined him $1000. It cost Matheson $1500 to take her case to the committee. It was a shallow victory but by then she had become aware of the bigger problem.

This is where Sandra Coney comes in. Coney, by then a feminist and freelance journalist, had been investigating, with women's studies lecturer Phillida Bunkle, a tip-off about what she would later call a 'disastrous research programme' at National Women's. In 1984 she had obtained a copy of a paper that had just been published in the American journal *Obstetrics and Gynaecology*. It was called 'The Invasive Potential of Carcinoma in Situ of the Cervix' and was about a study that had been carried out at National Women's since 1955 to examine the 'natural history of CIS of the cervix'.

The paper was written by whistle-blowing National Women's doctors Bill McIndoe, Jock McLean and Ronald Jones. It revealed Green's failed experiment. The authors had defied the convention of loyalty to the hospital and their senior colleagues to publish it. They hadn't even given a copy to hospital management until immediately prior to publication.

Ronald Jones wrote in 2009 that Green's study was 'the saddest and most shameful episode in New Zealand's medical history. The events reflect a basic human frailty, the reluctance of people to stand up against injustice and powerful individuals.'

However, the bombshell of a paper was roundly ignored by the medical establishment, to the frustration of its authors. Other doctors at the hospital even told Coney that its conclusions were wrong.

Fortunately, Coney and Bunkle weren't easily put off. Even before the whistle blowers' paper was published, they'd started searching for enough evidence to go to the media with the story. Given the secrecy surrounding the medical establishment, it wasn't easy. Though they had the paper, they hadn't managed to track down any of the affected patients. The breakthrough came via a mutual friend of Coney and Matheson. Knowing Matheson's medical history, the woman procured a copy of the paper from Coney and gave it to Matheson.

By that time Matheson had obtained a copy of her files from the hospital. This was no easy task. Their release was at the discretion of the hospital's medical superintendent, who had insisted Matheson give a good reason for daring to request her own records. Matheson lied: she said she was thinking of taking a compensation case to ACC. The files were alarming: they revealed Green's apparent mismanagement of her case. But when the journal paper landed on her desk she finally saw the bigger picture.

'Everything suddenly fell into place. I had been used like a laboratory rat. I realised too that there would be scores of other women who had no idea their lives were in danger. It was extremely frightening . . . The other realisation that hit me when I read the article was that the medical fraternity throughout the world knew of Green's programme at National Women's and had remained silent.'

Matheson contacted Coney and offered to hand over her hospital files. Though she had reservations about revealing such deeply personal information, she felt she had a responsibility to other women who might be unaware of the danger they were still in. As Coney and Bunkle read Matheson's file, all the pieces fell into place.

After years of research, Coney and Bunkle published an article in *Metro* magazine in June 1987 exposing the affair, and using Matheson's story, with her identity disguised, as a crucial part of their evidence. (Matheson later publicly revealed her identity.)

The furore that erupted over the article prompted Prime Minister David Lange to immediately launch a commission of inquiry into the study, to be headed by Judge Silvia Cartwright. Matheson was the first of twelve patients to testify during the six-month hearing, which began in August 1987. Cartwright had private interviews with another 70 patients and reviewed the cases of 1200 more. Medical experts and staff testified, including Green. Coney also testified.

As well as examining the CIS study, the inquiry also revealed that Green had ordered smears to be taken from newborn girls at National Women's in the 1960s, without their parents' knowledge or consent. In a three-year period 2244 girls were subjected to the tests, even though Green lost interest after the first year. Green had also preserved in wax more than 200 reproductive organs of baby girls who'd been stillborn or had died soon after birth—all without consent.

It also emerged that medical students at the hospital practised vaginal examinations and the fitting of intrauterine devices on anaesthetised women without their knowledge or consent.

In July 1988, Judge Cartwright reported back. The CIS study, she said, had been based on a theory that lacked scientific validity and little attention had been given to ethical considerations. The safeguards accepted by the doctors who had approved the study were 'illusory' and the concerns raised by Dr McIndoe and others 'counted for nothing'. The treatment of some patients was inadequate and consequently some women died. Before she reported back, Cartwright gave the government a list of names of women in the study who could still be unaware they might be in danger.

Cartwright's recommendations were far-reaching. She called for patients' rights to be enshrined in legislation, an overhaul of the medical disciplinary system, a national cervical screening programme and a rigorous system of ethical review. In 2008 Health and Disability Commissioner Ron Paterson–whose job was formed as a result of Cartwright's recommendations–said in a speech that her report 'led to a seismic shift in the patient–doctor relationship in New Zealand'.

Even two decades after the report, the study's ramifications were still being revealed. An analysis of Green's patients published in 2008 found that those who Green had chosen to treat conservatively–by not removing the abnormal tissue–were 30 times more likely to develop cancer in the 30 years that followed than women who were adequately treated.

Matheson is now retired and in her seventies. She and eighteen other patients received a million dollar settlement in 1992, after filing actions against the Auckland Area Health Board, the University of Auckland, Green, Bonham and the former superintendent of the hospital. The following year fifteen women received accident compensation for medical misadventure.

Bonham, who was heavily criticised in the fallout from the affair, took early retirement in 1988. In 1990 the Medical Council found him guilty of disgraceful conduct and censured and fined him. Green was judged too ill to face disciplinary action.

He died in 2001, aged 84.

It's impossible to know how many women developed cancer as a direct result of Green's inadequate treatment. Coney wrote in 2009: 'One of the most compelling pieces of evidence in the Cartwright Report is an appendix. It is a chart showing the development of invasive cancer in women who were treated for CIS at National Women's Hospital. Between the start of Green's trials and the mid-1970s when he stopped recruiting women, there is a dramatic spike in cases of invasive cancer. It is stark, tragic, an austere depiction of so much human misery.'

Cartwright herself wrote: 'For a minority of women, their management resulted in persisting disease, the development of invasive cancer and, in some cases, death.' Another woman whose CIS went untreated died in 1991, and yet another was diagnosed with invasive cervical cancer that year.

Without the persistence of Matheson, Coney and Bunkle, the study might never have come to the public's attention, and the conditions of women who'd unknowingly been left untreated might have deteriorated further.

Matheson has credited Bunkle and Coney for 'their tenacity and bravery in research and exposing the programme'. Bunkle, in turn, praised Matheson: 'The story could not have been told without her determination to see it through to whatever conclusion it may have.'

David Lange
Marilyn Waring

Anti-nuclear power brokers

One wintry night in 1962 a teenage law student was walking home from his bus stop in Otahuhu, South Auckland, when he noticed an eerie glow in the sky. From the northern horizon brilliant shafts of red and white light were spinning and mingling high in the atmosphere.

'I was arrested with awe as the sky pulsated,' he wrote later. 'I couldn't reason away the chill sweat of dread.'

About 100 kilometres to the south and 13 years later, a 23-year-old music student and part-time parliamentary researcher had just—to her surprise—been elected as National's member of parliament in Raglan. Her elderly predecessor, Doug Carter, took her aside for a quiet word to help her ease into political life.

'All sorts of people will give you all kinds of advice,' he said, 'but at the end of each day . . . the only person you have to live with is yourself.'

Each was a seminal moment in the young lives of two people who would go on to play a major part in New Zealand's response to the threat of nuclear armaments in the Pacific.

The young woman was Marilyn Waring, who nine years later would cross the floor to vote against her own party on nuclear-free legislation, knowing she was highly likely to bring down her own government and incur the wrath of her party's formidable leader, Prime Minister Sir Robert Muldoon.

The law student was David Lange, the Labour politician who would succeed Muldoon as prime minister and defy even his own advisors and New Zealand's closest allies to take a stand on the nuclear issue.

The lights he'd seen in the sky on that 1962 night were the atmospheric aftershocks of a one megaton nuclear weapon laced with millions of copper threads that had been exploded by the United States above Johnston Island in the North Pacific.

'The confusion in the sky that night haunted me as a vision of a man-made apocalypse,' Lange wrote later in his book *Nuclear Free–the New Zealand Way*, 'a terrifying retaliation of natural forces against the evil of unnatural invasion and a warning that a small country at the edge of the world in the South Pacific was no longer far enough away from the quarrels of the great powers to escape their consequences . . . I was struck by the conviction that the planet's future depended on our eliminating any possibility of nuclear war.'

At the time there was little the doctor's son could do about it, though that year he took a job clerking at a small Auckland law firm whose clients included the Communist Party of New Zealand. The party was then the loudest voice in the otherwise fairly muted local campaign against nuclear weapons. Lange found himself distributing leaflets protesting against American and French nuclear testing in the Pacific, marching in 'ban-the-bomb' rallies and attending public meetings. Though he sympathised with the cause, Lange was no communist and found the party's protest methods to be 'dismally unsuccessful'.

Still, by the early 1970s the anti-nuclear cause had gained some traction. It had entered the official policy statements of the Labour Party, which was elected to government in 1972. The new

Labour government sent two navy frigates, HMNZS *Canterbury* and HMNZS *Otago*, to the French test zone at Mururoa to draw worldwide attention to the issue, challenged the testing programme at the International Court of Justice, and proposed to the United Nations a South Pacific nuclear-free zone.

But the party's reign was short-lived. In 1975 Muldoon and National swept to power—and swept the anti-nuclear campaign off the agenda. Like many in the establishment—and the general populace—at that time, Muldoon was more concerned with keeping the United States on side and preserving the ANZUS defence alliance between New Zealand, Australia and the United States. The alliance was seen by many, including Muldoon, as our best defence against Soviet aggression.

Others, including Waring and Lange, doubted New Zealand was at risk from the Russians and were, to use Waring's word, 'aghast' at the commonly espoused deterrence theory—that harbouring nuclear weapons actually defused the possibility of nuclear war because an enemy would be reluctant to attack a country that was nuclear-armed.

'There is only one thing as terrifying as the nuclear weapon pointed in your direction,' Lange once said, 'and that is the nuclear weapon pointed in the enemy's direction: the outcome of their use would be the same in either case . . . annihilation of all of us.'

For New Zealand, the nuclear debate could have remained a theoretical argument. As an isolated country that was unlikely to become a target for a bomb, and didn't have the will or resources to become a big player in nuclear weapons development, New Zealand could have simply made an essentially token declaration of being nuclear-free with no practical consequences.

But the sticking point was New Zealand's relationship with the United States. The ANZUS treaty, signed by New Zealand, Australia and the United States in 1951, provided many New Zealanders with a sense of comfort and security in an era when it had become clear that Britain was in no position to defend its former colony. By the early 1970s, the treaty in practice meant little more than the odd exercise between the three countries' defence forces and the occasional visit to New Zealand ports by a US warship seeking a rest stop. But it was those visits that exploded the issue into the international spotlight.

The United States had a staunch policy of refusing to disclose whether its warships were nuclear powered or carried nuclear weapons. For New Zealand to be avowedly nuclear-free it would have to convince the US to change that policy, or ban American warships from its waters. And the US was not prepared to do the former, or stand for the latter.

Muldoon wasn't game to play hardball with the US. In 1976 he invited two US warships of undisclosed nuclear status to enter New Zealand harbours. Both vessels powered into Auckland Harbour surrounded by protest ships. Lange didn't sail out with the protest flotilla—'although I'm fairly buoyant, I had no sailing experience', he said—but did later defend in court Phillip Amos, a former Labour minister who was charged with obstruction for his part in the protest.

By the time the man's case came up for appeal before the Supreme Court (which threw it out), Lange had left the law to enter politics. In 1976 he won the seat of Mangere for Labour in a by-election. His time on the sidelines was coming to an end.

In the years to come, as the sharp and articulate Lange rose through Labour's parliamentary ranks, Waring found herself more and more at odds with the National Party and its domineering leader, especially on the nuclear issue. At the same time, the New Zealand public was beginning to come round to the nuclear-free cause.

From 1981, when National was re-elected with a majority of one,

Waring was, in her words, 'driven by the nuclear issue', and saw National's slim majority as an opportunity. 'I had from December 1981 worked out exactly what I would do,' she recalled later. 'I would cause an election on nuclear-free New Zealand. It took two and a half years to plan it.'

Her first chance came the following year when Labour MP Richard Prebble introduced a private member's bill calling for New Zealand to be declared a nuclear-free zone. But she bided her time. In return for voting against it—to the general disappointment of anti-nuclear campaigners—she negotiated the establishment of a parliamentary Disarmament and Arms Control Select Committee, which she believed was a more influential forum for the anti-nuclear issue.

Whether it was or not became a moot point. By 1983 she was prepared to draft her own bill on the anti-nuclear issue. In the end she didn't have to. In mid-1984 Prebble introduced another anti-nuclear bill. Waring sensed the time was right. She ignored threats from the party leadership and crossed the floor to vote for it, knowing Muldoon would be incensed. The bill was lost by one vote but Waring had made her stand. With another anti-nuclear bill due to be reported back to the House within the month, Muldoon knew his government was in a precarious position. He used Waring as an excuse to call an early election. It was just as she had intended.

Lange, by then leader of the Labour Party, was impressed by Waring's actions. 'Bravely she defied Muldoon,' he wrote later, 'an action requiring considerable courage in a caucus cowed by his overbearing personality . . . I found it appalling that Muldoon chose to make Marilyn Waring a scapegoat. She stood true to her convictions and voted in accordance with them.'

Historian Barry Gustafson detailed Waring's standoff with Muldoon in his biography of the former prime minister, *His Way*. He wrote that Muldoon subjected Waring to 'prolonged and severe' abuse. Shortly before the prime minister called the snap election he summoned her to his office, grumbling to his chief whip, Don McKinnon, that she was at times 'unhinged mentally and emotionally' and complaining, 'I don't know really how I can go on governing the country with a girl like this.'

When she arrived he apparently greeted her with words to the effect of: 'You perverted little liar. What the f*** do you think you're up to now?' To which she replied: 'Those words leave your lips again and I'll sue the shit out of you.'

While Waring sat with her feet on his coffee table and crunched on an apple to provoke him—as Gustafson tells it—Muldoon launched into an 'almost vindictive monologue'. The discussion was heated. At times Waring wept. At one point Muldoon told her, 'You have paraded out there as a saint, you're a pinnacle, you look clean, and I know you're not.'

But she refused to give in to his bullying and eventually left. After a few more drinks, Muldoon called the early election. It handed power—and the opportunity to make a move on the anti-nuclear issue—to David Lange.

As leader of the opposition, Lange had assumed that New Zealand would ban nuclear weapons as soon as Labour was elected. But there were complications. For starters, there was his view that the country should make a distinction between nuclear weapons, which he opposed, and propulsion, which he didn't. This put him at odds with most anti-nuclear proponents in New Zealand and he came in for heavy criticism from those who saw nuclear development in general as an environmental threat and wanted the country to make a stand against it.

He came to realise that the two issues were too closely linked in the minds of most New Zealanders. Eventually, in his words, he 'bowed to the inevitable and accepted that there were to be no qualifications on our nuclear-free policy'.

Which brought him to problem number two—the relationship with the United States. Though Lange was not prepared to bow on the issue of nuclear-armed ships, he had been prepared to reach a compromise with the US Government for the sake of preserving bilateral relations and ANZUS, by allowing ships that were nuclear propelled but not nuclear armed into New Zealand harbours. But since he was unable to acknowledge the distinction he felt he had no argument to make, considering the larger country's black and white position. He tried nonetheless.

The United States started putting pressure on Lange within hours of his election victory. That night Australian Prime Minister Bob Hawke rang his new New Zealand counterpart for the standard congratulatory call, and then put touring US Secretary of State George Shultz on the line. After the usual pleasantries, Shultz said ominously that they had some 'things to talk about' when he arrived in Wellington a few days later. 'A frisson of apprehension prevented me from enjoying the rest of the evening,' Lange recalled.

Lange was convinced that Shultz's New Zealand visit was just a passive-aggressive public relations exercise. He believed Shultz was trying to put pressure on the incoming government by issuing a covert threat in press conferences that without nuclear ship visits the ANZUS treaty would not survive. In private the American was more restrained. He told Lange that nuclear vessels were an important component of New Zealand's defence.

'That's not consistent with our policy,' said Lange.

'That's something we'll have to work through,' Shultz replied.

In the months—and indeed years—that followed, the Reagan administration continued to put pressure on Lange, who continued to try to talk them round. American diplomats tried to convince him, in mostly subtle and sometimes patronising ways, that he was tearing the fabric of Western security by challenging their nuclear status, hinted that New Zealand's export industry could be harmed, and showed him top-secret satellite pictures purportedly demonstrating the build-up of armaments in the Soviet Union. One presentation was so long he fell asleep.

'I felt instinctively that it was nonsense,' said Lange, 'but you can sometimes stop believing in yourself when the people you thought were on your side are saying you're letting them down.'

It wasn't just the US that put diplomatic pressure on Lange, who was also minister of foreign affairs. Even his own advisors in the Ministry of Foreign Affairs repeatedly warned him that pursuing a nuclear-free policy would lead to a breakdown in relations with the United States and could have severe economic consequences.

Australian political leaders too tried to exert influence. Hawke sent a top secret letter to Lange in December 1984 to warn him that New Zealand should not insist on special treatment.

The following month US diplomatic pressure gave way to a direct challenge–in January 1985 the US applied to send the warship USS *Buchanan* to New Zealand. Though it was an elderly ship that wasn't nuclear powered and was unlikely to be carrying nuclear weapons, the Americans refused to confirm that. The Ministry of Foreign Affairs recommended it be allowed access to New Zealand ports.

The US State Department issued a statement: 'The denial of port access,' it declared, 'would be a matter of grave concern which goes to the core of our mutual obligations as allies.' The ANZUS treaty was evidently at stake.

But the ambiguity over the ship's nuclear weaponry was unacceptable to the New Zealand government. Lange believed that allowing its visit would be a surrender: 'To be true to our policy and ourselves the USS *Buchanan* had to be rejected.'

And rejected it was.

The Americans responded angrily. A low-level bureaucrat was despatched to inform Lange that military co-operation between the two countries was over, that the Pentagon would no longer invite New Zealand to confidential security briefings and its diplomats would have a hard time getting access to anyone important in Washington, though New Zealand remained–in name at least–a member of ANZUS. The US Navy commander in chief of the Pacific, Admiral William Crowe, lobbied for sanctions against New Zealand and told a Senate committee that New Zealand's stand was likely to increase the risk of nuclear war.

Margaret Thatcher also got in on the act. New Zealand's High Commissioner to London, Bill Young, was lectured to at length by the British prime minister, who called the situation a 'tragedy' and complained that the policy would also effectively exclude British warships. He reported back to his government: 'Never in my life have I been subjected to such a firm barrage.'

At a press conference, Thatcher declared to an American journalist: 'I am as disappointed as you are in the approach taken by the New Zealand prime minister.' A British admiral, Sir John Fieldhouse, even told Lange, 'You are inspiring communism in Africa.'

Around this time Lange was invited to a debate at Oxford University in England. He would be leading a team arguing that nuclear weapons were morally indefensible. Prominent US conservative Jerry Falwell would lead the opposing team. A note was swiftly despatched to Lange from the British government, warning that British ministers were 'concerned' that he was getting himself involved in what was a politically contentious issue in the United Kingdom, as well as dragging Britain into the ANZUS dispute, and were anxious about the damage the debate could do to British and alliance interests.

It read: 'The press are likely to represent what is said as an attack on NATO, as detrimental to the Western position on arms control, and as adding to the difficulties already faced by some European countries.'

Lange was even warned by the British High Commissioner to Wellington, Terence O'Leary, who delivered the note, that 'Margaret won't like it.' Lange reassured him that he was not planning to launch an attack on NATO's doctrines. 'I didn't like to say to him,' he wrote later, 'that the Note made me more determined than ever to go to Oxford.'

Lange's team won the debate and he became the instant darling of the international anti-nuclear movement for such comments as: 'It is self-defeating logic, just as the weapons themselves are self-defeating: to compel an ally to accept nuclear weapons against the wishes of that ally is to take the moral position of totalitarianism, which allows for no self-determination, and which is exactly the evil that we are supposed to be fighting against.'

The most famous moment of the debate was an unscripted one. When Falwell pressed Lange for an answer on whether New Zealand would remain in ANZUS, Lange said: 'And I'm going to give it to you if you hold your breath just for a moment . . . I can smell the uranium on it as you lean forward!'

Even Lange's political rival Jim Bolger, who became leader of the opposition the following year and prime minister in 1990, wrote later that Lange's performance had been outstanding. 'It was David Lange at his best—eloquent, penetrating and, when required, very witty. For the record, the motion was carried 298 to 250. Of much more enduring interest though, was that the profile of the anti-nuclear argument had been given a very big international audience.'

Lange was welcomed back to Auckland Airport by hundreds of supporters—and then drove straight to a butter factory where hundreds of farmers turned up to protest against his apparent disregard for the future of their exports.

Nevertheless, New Zealand's anti-nuclear policy was by then entrenched. On 8 June 1987, thanks in part to the efforts of Waring and Lange, The New Zealand Nuclear Free Zone, Disarmament, and Arms Control Act was passed, legalising the country's position as a nuclear-free zone. The United States officially suspended its ANZUS treaty obligations.

In 1990 Lange wrote that it was the ordinary people of New Zealand who made their country nuclear-free.

'I was in a government with a mandate from the electorate to take substantial steps to reduce the dangers to New Zealand of nuclear weapons. In putting that mandate into practice, I ran into many difficulties. Some were traps set for me by others. Some were totally self-inflicted. For all the problems I faced and all the false starts I made, I knew it was worth it. It felt right.'

George Shultz later became an anti-nuclear campaigner and admitted that he'd always been a big fan of New Zealand.

'New Zealand was always a wonderful country to work with. We had a little disagreement about nuclear things which strained the ANZUS alliance but I remember saying at the time, "We part, but we part as friends."'

Fred Hollows

Visionary doctor

One day in 1968 Fred Hollows got a life-changing phone call. Would he mind taking a look at a couple of Aboriginal men with eye trouble?

Donald Nangiari and Vincent Lingiari duly reported to his ophthalmology clinic at the Prince of Wales hospital in Sydney. They had myriad problems: one was blind in one eye and their three remaining eyes were dogged by cataracts, blocked ducts, pus, trachoma. And something else—a strange white hazing of the cornea the New Zealand-born doctor had never seen before.

He called in a colleague, Roger McGuinness. McGuinness took a look and, after a pause, said, 'That's Labrador keratopathy.'

Hollows was fascinated. It was a condition that until then had never been detected in Australia, in which the cornea is damaged by long exposure to the reflection of ultra-violet light from snow or sand. He subsequently operated and partially restored the men's sight.

The two men had been flown down from their home on a cattle station in the Northern Territory, and Hollows was told he was welcome to return with them, if he was willing to make himself useful. He eagerly accepted.

It took three days to get to the camp of the Gurindji people at Watti Creek. On the first night he slept under a tarpaulin. Next morning he examined the eyes of 30 men who'd served as stockmen.

They all had Labrador keratopathy from working for long hours in the harsh sun. Their hats didn't protect them, as the light was reflected off the ground.

'It wasn't a blinding condition but it impaired sight,' said Hollows later. 'As well, there were cataracts that were blinding them, and signs of advanced trachoma and other things . . . It was a shock to me. I'd been working at the hospital and in my private practice and seeing a parade of eye disorders, but nothing like this.'

He also examined the women and children and discovered that though they weren't afflicted with Labrador keratopathy, they were riddled with cataracts and trachoma, a condition that began as untreated conjunctivitis and could cause blindness. Trachoma thrived in unsanitary conditions and had been problematic in the early days of British settlement in Australia, but had all but disappeared in the European population as general health had improved.

'It was like something out of the medical history books–eye diseases of a kind and degree that hadn't been seen in western society for generations,' said Hollows 'The neglect this implied, the suffering and wasted quality of human life were appalling.'

Hollows, in his words, 'went wild'. He marched to the nearest station and commandeered a radio.

'I got on to Darwin and demanded that they send a doctor down to look at this situation. That was when I found out how things worked up here.'

They sent a man–Hollows doubted his medical credentials–who was utterly unmoved. The man got up on the back of a truck and embarked on a lecture berating the people for their bad health, telling them they'd have to go to the clinic at a station ten kilometres away. His audience did what they always did when somebody started shouting at them–they turned their backs on the man.

Hollows, who had moved to Australia three years previously,

was getting a terse introduction to Australian politics. The Gurindji people were pioneers of the Aboriginal land rights movement and were two years into what would become a seven-year strike. It started as a protest against their living conditions and meagre pay and escalated into an ultimately successful political campaign to have their land returned. Their leader was Lingiari, who was many years later appointed a Member of the Order of Australia.

Hollows concluded the lack of medical services was about teaching them a lesson. He flew back to Sydney and called a press conference, which he used to highlight the discrepancies between medical services–eye health in particular–between city and outback, Aborigines and white Australians.

Thus the eye doctor and teacher–who'd been born in Dunedin, raised in Palmerston North and educated at Victoria and Otago universities–became a campaigner. He devoted the rest of his life to improving the eyesight, and with it the lives, of underprivileged people throughout Australia and around the world. He had, said celebrated Australian author Frank Hardy, 'an awe-inspiring gut feeling against injustice, which put the fire of anger into the soul of the kindest man I ever met'.

Hollows' appeal to the press made headlines–and had more unsettling consequences. Not long after his outburst, he arrived at his Sydney home to find that two men in gabardine overcoats and hats had called, and asked his wife if it was the home of 'the Professor Hollows who's interested in native affairs'. She had curtly sent them away. By the look of them, and their car–which had a large rooftop aerial–she concluded they were agents from ASIO, Australia's secret service.

'I was ropeable,' wrote Hollows in his autobiography. 'All I'd done was examine a hundred and fifty blackfellows sitting by Watti Creek and found the amount of disease you'd need to look at a million and a half whites to discover, and talked about the differences. I hadn't incited rebellion or anything, and now here they were setting the bloody ASIO dogs on me . . . I thought: "What can I do to get back at the bastards?"'

His revenge was not what you might except of a specialist physician and university professor. He cast around for an illegal act that he could get away with. At midnight one night he threw a chain with a big hook on it, a chainsaw and some axes into his car boot, and set off with three acquaintances to the entrance to the Royal National Park in southern Sydney.

Lining the entrance was a series of advertising billboards. He had long been appalled that they were allowed to be sited on park land. The four men destroyed them with relish.

'All the hoardings had signs mounted on them informing the citizenry that anyone who interfered with this precious property would be fined $2000, gaoled for life . . . that sort of thing,' recalled Hollows. 'We put the signs very neatly in the middle of the shambles.'

The billboards were very quickly erected again, with stronger scaffolding. So again Hollows and his mates tore them down. They went up again. This time the little civil disobedience squad couldn't get them to budge. 'But we gave them a run for their money,' said Hollows.

The press conference had several other—more constructive—consequences. Hollows was asked to help set up a medical service for Aboriginal people in the poor Sydney suburb of Redfern. They'd long complained that they weren't welcome in doctors' surgeries or hospitals. It took ten days for the service to start operating, and it spurred the creation of dozens more nationwide.

Hollows' initial contribution was to plunder supplies from his hospital, from stethoscopes to drugs. 'We backed a truck up to the pharmacy at the hospital and loaded it half full—tens of thousands of dollars worth of pharmaceuticals.'

He didn't always have to swipe the supplies–plenty of medical staff were sympathetic, and he was swamped with offers to volunteer at the clinic. Hollows too volunteered as a GP, often paying out of his own pocket for his patients' prescriptions and other expenses. Like his experience in the Northern Territory, it was an eye-opener.

As well as dealing with poor general health and nutrition and a shortage of birth control that led to amateur abortions, he was constantly treating bruises and contusions, often the result of run-ins with the police.

His work in Redfern led him back to the outback. He was invited to join a medical team that was travelling up to Bourke, a remote town in northern New South Wales. They set up in a dusty showground and he started examining children's eyes. He found case after case of trachoma among the Aboriginal people, and none in the white Australians.

'I was very annoyed for humanitarian and professional reasons,' he later wrote. 'There was really no excuse for the complete non-detection of trachoma and I knew it meant that the Aborigines had to be living in sub-standard conditions.'

He went further into the desert, to a tiny settlement called Engonnia. More trachoma. With the help of a trailblazing English ophthalmologist, Barrie Jones, he set up a mass drug treatment programme. It began in Engonnia and eventually become a model for an Australian-wide assault, the National Trachoma and Eye Health Program, which was introduced in the late 1970s under the auspices of the Royal Australian and New Zealand College of Ophthalmologists. It probably wouldn't have happened without the publicity that Hollows generated.

The programme was launched, after a concerted campaign of political lobbying, with a $AU1.4 million government grant. Hollows stepped in from time to time to sort out opposition from the medical establishment.

Hollows took two years' leave from the hospital and university to become the programme's founding director. He set a simple ambitious goal: to eliminate tracomatous blindness from Australia. He also set the salaries—consequently his income took a nose-dive and he struggled to pay his mortgage.

In the first three years of the programme more than 100,000 people were screened in communities around Australia. In some communities in the Northern Territory and Western Australia 80 per cent of the population was infected with tracoma. About 27,000 people were treated, 1000 received operations and 7000 received glasses. Eighty ophthalmologists volunteered for the programme and locals were trained in eye care. Hollows worked in almost every state and territory, sometimes screening 500 children in a day. Though he had no qualms about being unpopular with bureaucrats, he became a legend among his patients for his rough-and-ready image, humility, straight talk and good humour.

'They said it was pure magic and it was,' said Hollows. 'For those people it was the first time that they could see that they were part of a process that was ameliorating human suffering in a direct one-to-one hands-on situation.

'I had plenty of misgivings and I'm sure we made mistakes. But I had great faith in the people I was working with and I was constantly seeing evidence that we were going about things the right way.'

Hollows' work took him to other parts of the world—Mexico, Burma, Thailand, Nepal, Eritrea, Vietnam. The work largely involved training local doctors to address typical third-world eye problems, chiefly trachoma and cataracts. He also became heavily involved in fundraising to build lens factories in Nepal, Eritrea and Vietnam to dramatically drive down the costs of intraocular lenses, which were vital to treating cataracts.

But then the man who'd helped to improve the health of

hundreds of thousands of people had to focus on himself. In 1989 he was diagnosed with a slow-moving but terminal kidney cancer. He interpreted it not as a cue to slow down, but to work even harder. There was still much to achieve.

'This threat, distressing though it is, adds piquancy and value to every day,' he wrote. 'Each day of survival is a small victory and I am resolved not to waste the winnings.'

As the disease took hold, Hollows worked flat out with his wife, Gabi, to set up a foundation in his name that would carry on his fundraising and development work. In the years before he died Australia loaded him up with honours. He was made a Companion of the Order of Australia and named 1990 Australian of the Year.

The citation for the latter honour remarked that the New Zealander once described as the 'intellectual with the wharfie's manner' had become an Australian folk hero, an iconoclast who inspired some and angered others.

He died at home in Sydney on 10 February 1993, surrounded by his wife and seven children, and was buried in Bourke. He was 63. The lens factories in Eritea, Nepal and Vietnam opened over the following two years.

An old friend and colleague, Susan Bennett, said Hollows died a real hero, 'whose heroism came not from a moment of glory or madness, but rather from the hard slog of running clinics in Bourke and across the country for years, from his vision of what could be achieved here in Australia and in Eritrea, Vietnam and Nepal, his refusal to be blocked by difficulties and his inspiration of others.'

4.

IDEALISTS

Te Whiti o Rongomai

Prince of peace

Colonel William Messenger was apprehensive as he approached the gates of Parihaka in Taranaki.

He'd been called down from his farm at Pukearuhe in North Taranaki to take charge of a contingent of 120 armed police in a raid on the Maori village. About 1600 government troops were surrounding the settlement, and cannons were trained on it. They'd been warned to expect trouble.

It was well known among Pakeha settlers that the elders of Parihaka were anxious for peace. They were led by prophets Te Whiti o Rongomai and Tohu Kakahi, who preached a message of non-violent resistance. But Messenger had heard that the young men of the 2500-strong village were planning to fight, that they'd been preparing for war in order to take back lands that had been confiscated. He had orders to fire at the slightest hint of resistance.

It was obvious the government was taking the assault on the village seriously–the native minister himself, John Bryce, was leading the charge, mounted on a white steed and in full military regalia. His mission was to disband the village and arrest its leaders.

Messenger was among the first of the troops to march, slowly but surely, on Parihaka, on 5 November 1881. He was amazed by what greeted him.

'There was a line of children across the entrance to the big village, a kind of singing class directed by an old man with a stick,' he said later. 'The children sat there unmoving, droning away, and even when a mounted officer galloped up and pulled his horse up so short that the dirt from its forefeet spattered the children they still went on chanting, perfectly oblivious, apparently, to the pakeha, and the old man calmly continued his monotonous drone.

'I was the first to enter the Maori town with my company. I found my only obstacle was the youthful feminine element. There were skipping parties of girls on the road. When I came to the first set of girls I asked them to move, but they took no notice. I took hold of one end of the skipping rope, and the girl at the other end pulled it away so quickly that it burnt my hands. At last, to make a way for my men, I tackled one of the rope-holders. She was a fat, substantial young woman, and it was all I could do to lift her up and carry her to one side of road. She made not the slightest resistance, but I was glad to drop the buxom wench.

'My men were all grinning at the spectacle of their captain carrying the big girl off. I marched them in at once through the gap and we were in the village.'

Once inside, the troops found the adults of the village sitting calmly before them, Te Whiti and Tohu among them. The women had been busy baking 500 loaves of bread to share with their expected visitors.

'Undisturbed quiet reigned among them,' read that day's entry in Swiss-born soldier Anton Fromme's diary. 'Had they given up all battle? Our calvary penetrated right up to them and gave them half an hour to hand over to us Te Whiti, Tohu and the 34 chiefs present. The half hour went by in undisturbed silence–no Maori stirred.'

Bryce, it was later reported, had formed plans for a grand gesture of advancing on Te Whiti on horseback and confronting him. But with the crush of people he was forced to walk.

As he approached, the prophet said, 'I have done nothing but peaceful work.' Te Whiti invited him to talk, but the minister ordered his arrest, and that of other key figures. Fromme was among the troops who moved in.

'All surrendered without offering the slightest resistance,' he later wrote. 'We tied their hands behind their backs and led them out of the village, with the Maoris looking on; we loaded them on to a cart, and sent them, under strong cavalry escort to the prison in New Plymouth. Strange! No Maori stirred when the chiefs were led away.'

Even as Te Whiti was taken away, his hands tied, he is said to have urged his people to remain passive. 'Even if the bayonet be put to your breasts do not resist . . . be not sorry but turn away the sorrowful heart this day . . . we looked for peace and we find war. Be forbearing, patient and steadfast, keep to peaceful works. Be not dismayed, and have no fear for the ultimate result.'

A *Lyttleton Times* newspaper reporter who had crept up to watch the scene, despite Bryce's order that journalists be kept away, wrote, 'The whole spectacle was saddening in the extreme; it was an industrious, law-abiding, moral, and hospitable community calmly awaiting the approach of the men sent to rob them of everything dear to them.'

Far worse was to come. After the leaders were taken away, the troops sat down to a midday meal. Rum was handed out. They then searched the houses in the village for weapons and set up guard posts around the village.

According to Fromme's diary, the troops were then given free time, but were warned to keep their revolvers at the ready and not touch any Maori property.

'We found the latter order too difficult to obey,' he said.

In fact the entire village was looted and many of the houses destroyed. Messenger recalled: 'Many of our Government men stole greenstones and other treasures from the native houses; among them were some fine meres.'

It didn't stop there. The village had a thriving garden and small farm. Fromme noted: 'There were masses of pigs, geese, ducks and other fowl running around the village. We had set out this morning, full of the joy of battle, and had not the slightest opportunity to show how brave we might be. We, therefore, let our bloodthirstiness reign over the pigs and fowl.'

The Waitangi Tribunal later noted there was 'evidence that women were raped and otherwise molested'.

Over the next few weeks about 1600 of the village's people were forcibly evicted. Some were taken away by train to other parts of the region and just left at the station, with orders not to return to Parihaka. Six hundred were allowed to remain, under the close supervision of the armed constabulary.

The charges against Te Whiti were that he had been, 'wickedly, maliciously, and seditiously contriving and intending to disturb the peace'. A trial held in New Plymouth proved inconclusive but, instead of being released, the two prophets remained in custody for six months before being transferred to the South Island. There they were incarcerated before being taken on a lengthy tour of the island, designed to convince them of the wonders of Pakeha technology. In reality it was just an excuse to keep them out of the way while Parihaka was laid to ruin.

Te Whiti and Tohu were unimpressed by what they were being shown and continued to call for a trial or release. The government finally let them out in 1883 and they were escorted back to what was left of Parihaka.

Te Whiti had been a young man when his Te Atiawa hapu had moved to Parihaka. War was then raging between British settler forces and Maori throughout much of the North Island. The colonists had confiscated massive amounts of land from Maori and this dispossession prompted the tangata whenua to fight back.

From a very young age Te Whiti was identified as being a future teacher and prophet. His elders ensured that he inherited as much of their knowledge as they could impart. As he grew older, he combined his traditional spiritual knowledge with a deep study of the Bible and a commitment to Christian principles. Te Whiti weaved together these two strands of spiritual belief and developed his own doctrine that manifested itself as his policy of peaceful resistance.

Having accompanied Maori war parties on skirmishes against the British in 1860, Te Whiti—who carried a tokotoko (walking stick) instead of a weapon—had seen war first hand. This only served to reinforce his belief that meeting violence with violence was not the best way to resolve anything.

Along with Tohu, Te Whiti began to preach a policy of resistance through non-violent action. They condemned greed, violence and drunkenness. The use of weapons was outlawed under any circumstances. 'Guns and powder,' said the prophet, 'shall no longer be the protection of man. Our weapon is forbearance, patience, non-resistance. God is our refuge and our strength.' His message was that Pakeha should respect Maori land ownership and acknowledge the independence of Maori.

Tohu and Te Whiti were condemned as fanatics by the colonial powers, who found the concept of peaceful resistance unsettling. Even more confusing for them must have been the adoption of the white feather as an emblem of the peace movement at Parihaka. For the colonial soldiers, a white feather was a sign of cowardice. Tohu is believed to have had a vision of an albatross flying down to the village. He believed this was a sign from the Holy Spirit sanctioning the peace movement. From then on, a single white albatross feather became emblematic of Parihaka and its ideals.

In the late 1860s, Te Whiti established regular monthly meetings at Parihaka. These meetings always fell on the eighteenth day of the month, as a commemoration of 18 March 1860, the day on which fighting broke out between Maori and Pakeha in Waitara. These meetings were a forum for Maori and Pakeha leaders to discuss the injustices being brought upon Taranaki Maori and to devise peaceful strategies to prevent further land grabs. Never swerving from his ideals of peace and non-violence, Te Whiti acquired followers from throughout the North Island. Some former warriors found it difficult not to react to aggression with violence but their respect for Te Whiti's mana was such that they followed his lead.

In 1879 the government began to survey 6500 hectares of confiscated land on the Waimate Plain. The government had promised that reserves would be set aside for Maori but the promise was broken. Te Whiti demanded that the reserves be included in the survey but he was ignored. He decided to look for other ways to make his voice heard.

One of the forms of peaceful resistance devised by Te Whiti involved sending his people out to disrupt the surveyors. This disruption involved blocking roads, pulling up survey pegs and ploughing confiscated land. When Te Whiti's men were arrested, they were instructed to put up no resistance, no matter what kind of treatment was meted out to them.

This unusual behaviour and the unwillingness of Te Whiti's followers to resort to violence drew the attention of magistrates and politicians. John Bryce became increasingly concerned that Parihaka was becoming a 'headquarters of fanaticism and disaffection'. A bill was passed allowing any arrested protesters to be held without trial. Thousands of Te Whiti's followers were arrested and found themselves sent into exile in the South Island, where they were forced to work in building infrastructure. The conditions in which they lived were horrendous—caves that some of them were forced to live in can be seen to this day carved into the cliffs in Dunedin's

Andersons Bay. Many didn't make it back to Taranaki alive.

Despite these measures, the Parihaka movement continued aforce. Bryce decided it was time for stronger tactics. Taranaki was home to huge numbers of soldiers and there were stockades and forts everywhere so it wasn't difficult to gather a considerable force for the invasion of Parihaka. Though the attack broke up the village for several years, Bryce could not break Te Whiti's spirit.

After Te Whiti and Tohu were finally allowed to return to the village, they continued to promote resistance through peaceful means, though the fierceness with which the government had dealt with the movement in 1881 meant that it never regained its huge following.

Had Te Whiti not been so respected as a prophet and teacher, there would have been much more bloodshed in Taranaki in the 1880s. Te Whiti has come to be revered as a man of peace and a visionary. His life is perhaps summed up best in his own words to his followers just before his arrest in 1881: 'Though I am killed, yet I shall live. The future is mine and little children will answer in the future when questioned as to the author of peace, "Te Whiti," and I will bless them.'

Te Whiti died in 1907. His age was not known. At his tangi, parliamentarian Sir Maui Pomare spoke passionately about his legacy. Pomare, the first Maori doctor, was a child of the village of Parihaka when it was invaded and bore a permanent reminder. His foot had been trampled by a constabulary horse and he walked with a limp for the rest of his life.

'Depart to the illustrious chiefs who have gone before, to thy brave comrades of old, to the Giver of war and peace,' Pomare said. 'Go to that land from which no man ever returned. Thy words have come true; the lips of children speak of thee as "the man of peace and goodwill to all people, on the West Coast". In thine own words thou said'st that war and peace, as life and death, were foreordained. The sun was overshadowed at times with many troubled clouds, but thy sun has sunk gloriously in the west, leaving thy people disconsolate.'

Richard Henry

Conservationist

In 1975 a single male kakapo was discovered living in Fiordland's remote Gulliver Valley. With kakapo at extreme risk of extinction, finding a new bird was always going to be cause for celebration but finding this little bloke was even more special. He is thought to be the last of the mainland Fiordland kakapo.

Most surviving kakapo are from the Steward Island population. As the number of birds has dwindled the risk of interbreeding has grown. Finding a new male from a genetically distinct group would provide crucial genetic diversity for the kakapo breeding programme and help this most endearing of our native birds survive.

When the time came to give the bachelor bird a name, there could be none more appropriate than Richard Henry. Both the bird and the man he was named after were Fiordland lads who helped save the kakapo from extinction.

While Richard Henry, the kakapo, was moved to Maud Island where he sired offspring, his namesake's lovelife was not quite so straightforward. Richard Henry, whose family emigrated from Ireland to Australia when he was six, arrived in New Zealand in 1874 as a 21-year-old. Always an outdoorsman, he soon came to love the rugged country of the South Island. He moved around frequently, taking jobs in whatever spot took his fancy. Work was plentiful and he stayed in each place until he felt like moving on. During his first years in New Zealand he worked as a bushman, in sawmills and on gold claims.

His first conservation mission was an attempt to eliminate rabbits that were threatening to take over hard-won Southland and Otago farms. The introduced pests were swarming across the paddocks and farmers employed men like Henry to shoot them. While he worked to control rabbits, he began to formulate ideas on how best to control other invading pests. He also took great pleasure in observing native birds and their habitats.

While he was working as a rabbit shooter in Northern Southland, Henry heard that the Wakatipu Steam Navigation Company was looking for men to help build its steamship, the *Mountaineer*, in nearby Kingston. Henry was an experienced carpenter, so he took on the job and moved to Kingston in 1878. Over the next couple of years he is thought to have met and fallen in love with a woman who he hoped to marry. When the object of his affections rejected him, he retreated to the solitude of Fiordland, settling on the shores of Lake Te Anau. He built himself a hut, thought to have been the first dwelling on the site of the Te Anau township, and set about making himself indispensable to local farmers.

Although his chosen home was remote, there were a handful of runholders in the area who were happy to have such a capable worker available and Henry had no shortage of occupations, from boatman to bush guide, from sawmiller to shepherd and pretty much everything in between.

Henry enjoyed the somewhat spasmodic nature of his work as it meant that, when he felt the need, he could go bush. He'd take his dog, hop in his boat and sail across the lake before disappearing into the mountains for weeks on end. While he was out in the wilderness he studied the birdlife. He was particularly interested in ground birds, such as kakapo, weka and kiwi, so during his time in the bush he observed their behaviour closely, becoming particularly knowledgeable about kakapo breeding patterns.

While on these trips he made extensive notes about the birds and kept tallies of their numbers. He was distressed to discover the bird numbers were declining and predicted that kakapo would become extinct if action was not taken to save them. Ironically, this decline was brought about by the introduction to New Zealand of mustelids–such as stoats and ferrets–to try to control the rabbit population.

Around this time a Canterbury naturalist, Thomas Potts, put forward the idea that 'considerable areas of land should be set aside and held under tapu as to dog and gun'. One of the areas he suggested was Resolution Island in Dusky Sound.

The Otago Acclimatisation Society, whose members included Te Anau runholder Edward Melland, supported Potts' idea. Melland was a good friend of Henry and was aware of his interest.

When the island was proclaimed a reserve in 1891, Henry was the obvious choice to become the sanctuary's first caretaker. Henry, by then in his mid-forties, understood the urgency of the task at hand as bird populations continued to be wiped out. He was keen to move onto the island and start rescuing birds. Bureaucracy, however, didn't understand the urgency. Efforts to find funding for the sanctuary moved at glacial pace.

The constant delays and a bout of ill health made Henry lament what he viewed as his lack of achievement in life. As a result, he settled his affairs in Te Anau and headed to Auckland in the hope of convincing the city's scientists that the native bird populations were in a perilous state.

His campaign fell on deaf ears, and the rejection made him question his future as a naturalist. He figured he was too old to go back to working in sawmills or as a bushman and convinced himself there was only one way out. With his revolver, he attempted to shoot himself twice in the head. The first bullet deflected off his skull and embedded itself in his scalp and the second bullet failed to fire. In typically practical Henry fashion, he walked to Auckland Hospital and admitted himself.

Before long Melland heard of his friend's misfortune and sent word that the conservationists had finally agreed to appoint a curator on Resolution Island. He asked Henry if he would like to apply for the job and Henry replied with a resounding 'yes'. Three weeks after his suicide attempt, Henry was on his way back to his beloved Fiordland with a renewed sense of purpose.

Six other people applied for the job as curator of Resolution Island but Henry was a shoe-in. No one else had his local knowledge or his depth of understanding of the birds. The job paid £123 a year and he was supplied with a five metre dinghy and the materials to build a small house, boatshed and slipway.

In July 1894, the steamer Hinemoa delivered Henry to Pigeon Island, where he set up camp and took to the task of populating neighbouring Resolution Island with birds from the mainland. Even the people who'd given Henry the job weren't sure whether the birds would survive being relocated. But from his years of observing their behaviour, Henry was confident that they would, given the right conditions. He was proved right.

Henry relocated some 750 kakapo and kiwi to island sanctuaries within Dusky Sound over the next six years. To do this he sailed his dinghy—which he called Putangitangi, the Maori name for the paradise shelduck—across the Sound to the mainland. Once there he used his dog to help track and trap the birds. Using a predator to trap endangered birds must have seemed odd to conservationists at the time but Henry had trained his companion well and ensured that the dog always wore a bell, so Henry could follow it, and a muzzle, so it wouldn't harm the birds.

The bird population of Resolution Island and the other island sanctuaries established by Henry soon began to thrive and by 1898 he was focusing his energy on monitoring the birds that he had relocated rather than searching for more birds to move.

In early 1900, Henry's hard work to save the kakapo and kiwi of Fiordland was dealt a harsh blow. Visitors to the island on the schooner *Cavalier* told him that they had seen a weka being chased down the beach by a weasel. Henry responded in disbelief but over the coming weeks the significance of this sighting filled him with unease—could all his work have been in vain?

On 4 August, the terrible truth became only too clear when he saw a weasel with his own eyes. Depressed at the thought all his hard work would come to nothing, he quickly set up an eradication programme. But Henry was unable to stave off the tide of invaders preying on his beloved birds. Once the predators had become established on the island it was pointless for Henry to continue his work there. In 1908, he left his sanctuary for good.

The birds on Resolution Island were slowly massacred and Henry died, lonely and depressed, in an Auckland psychiatric hospital in 1929. He regarded his experiment as a failure, but in fact his observations on kakapo behaviour, booming and breeding habits proved to be indispensable to rangers trying to save the breed from extinction in the coming years.

His pioneering work in using dogs to track birds and in successfully transferring endangered bird populations also gave those who took over the task of saving the kakapo a massive head start. Henry is credited as being the grandfather of the New Zealand conservation movement. Without Richard Henry, the man, the chances of Richard Henry, the bird, saving his species would have been greatly diminished.

Archibald Baxter
Mark Briggs

Peace lovers

They called it the 'crucifixion'.

In a desolate yard at Mud Farm, a prison camp near the World War I battleground of Ypres, Otago farmer Archibald Baxter was tied fast by his ankles, knees and wrists to a leaning wooden pole. He couldn't move a millimetre. The ropes were so tight that they cut into his flesh and his hands were black with congested blood. His arms were cramping from the effort of supporting almost all of his weight. The temperature was below zero but he wore no coat. Snow was clinging to him and an icy gale stung his face.

Through the blizzard he could see the prison guards in their hut, warming themselves at a red-hot stove. The smell of coffee wafted out. A deadly numbness crept up until it reached his heart. He feared that every breath would be his last. Everything grew black.

One afternoon later that month—March 1918—Baxter stood beside the bunk of a friend, Manawatu flax worker Mark Briggs. Briggs, like Baxter, was in his mid-thirties but his face was as pale and shrunken as that of an old man. A deep flesh wound covered much of his lower back. Dirt had been ground into it so deeply it couldn't be removed without hospital treatment, which he'd been denied. He had also been refused blankets. He was in indescribable agony. His hut was so close to the Belgian front line that shells flew through the air around it.

'You've had a rough time,' Baxter said.

It was an understatement. That morning a cable wire had been wound around Briggs' chest under his arms, and four men had used it to drag him along a duck walk—a rough footpath through the mud to the front line, constructed of planks with battens nailed across it at short intervals. The nails, battens and wire had ripped off his clothing and torn into his flesh.

At one point the men had pulled him through a shell crater full of icy water. When he'd reached the bank they'd picked him up by his shoulders and tipped him back in, head over heels. He'd managed to right himself and stand. One of the men had said, 'Drown yourself now, you bastard.' By the time they relented they'd dragged him about a kilometre. He was unable to stand and was shaking uncontrollably from shock.

Baxter and Briggs each spent two years as prisoners of war. But their captors—and torturers—weren't Germans or Turks. They were Allied servicemen following the orders of the New Zealand authorities. As well as being subjected to the 'crucifixion', the two men were beaten, denied food and medical attention, publicly stripped naked, doused with freezing water, clamped in irons and handcuffs, court-martialled, locked up in solitary confinement, publicly paraded and jeered at, threatened with execution and left for dead—simply because they didn't believe in violence and refused to become part of the war killing machine. Their mistreatment is one of the greatest injustices in New Zealand history. And their resolve to stand by their convictions in the face of torture, humiliation and privation is one of the country's greatest acts of bravery.

Both men were called up under conscription in 1917 to serve as soldiers but because of their beliefs they refused to take any orders. Baxter was a committed pacifist and believed all war was wrong.

Briggs was a socialist and militant unionist who objected to the ordinary man being forced to fight a war at the behest of the whims of political leaders and in the interests of industrialists.

Public and political sentiment wasn't on their side. A fervour of imperial patriotism had gripped the country. Newspapers labelled objectors 'shirkers', 'traitors' and 'parasites'. The women's pro-war White Feather League accosted men who weren't serving, and posted them white feathers, representing cowardice.

The government line was that objectors could be excused only if they belonged to certain religious groups that could prove their tenets regarded war as 'contrary to divine revelation'. In practice, this was restricted to Quakers, Christadelphians and Seventh Day Adventists. Of about 800 men who appealed against conscription on conscientious grounds, just 73 were exempted. The others were coerced into serving overseas and/or imprisoned in New Zealand and forced to do hard labour.

Baxter's opposition to war was so well known that the authorities didn't even bother sending him a call-up notice. Two policemen ambushed him outside his family farm in Brighton in February 1917 and took him to Kensington Drill Hall in Dunedin, where they handed him to military authorities. He was marched through the streets by four guards armed with rifles with bayonets fixed, before being locked in a cell at the St Kilda Battery.

He was transported to Wellington the following day and spent the next four months imprisoned at the Trentham Military Camp, the Terrace Jail, Mount Cook Prison and the Alexandra Barracks. He consistently refused to take any military orders and refused to do hard labour.

Mark Briggs was arrested in March 1917 after ignoring orders to report for an army medical examination. He also spent several months bouncing between Trentham, Mount Cook Prison and the Terrace Jail.

After dark on 13 July, Briggs and seven other objectors were marched by military escort through the streets of Wellington. As the wharf came into sight, with the *Waitemata* troop ship lying in wait, they realised the authorities had come up with a new plan: to quietly transport them to war. They were given no chance to farewell their families.

The men were forced up the gangway and down into the ship's small clink. The following morning the door opened again and Baxter was shoved inside, along with two of his brothers, Jack and Sandy, and another man. By the time the ship pulled out from the wharf later that day fourteen objectors were confined to the small room: Briggs and the three Baxters, Fred Adin, Garth Ballantyne, David Gray, Thomas Harland, Lawrence Kirwan, William Little, Daniel Maguire, Henry Patton, Lewis Penwright and Albert Sanderson. By the war's end 170 conscientious objectors had been shipped to Europe from New Zealand.

A few days after the *Waitemata* had sailed, Minister of Defence James Allen said the men had been deported to give them another chance to do their duty, and they would be offered non-combatant work. He hoped the different circumstances would induce them to change their minds. He expressed surprise that they had been deported without their parents' knowledge and reassured a deputation including the mother of 21-year-old Garth Ballantyne that they would be subjected to no persecution during the voyage to England.

In fact the persecution began within days. When the men refused to put on uniforms they were lined up on the deck in front of hundreds of soldiers and officers, stripped naked one by one and forcibly dressed in uniform. They were also forced to have haircuts. When Briggs objected he was dragged upstairs, his heels crashing against the steps, and held down by six men. His head ended up covered in cuts.

The men had already faced harsh punishment in prison but they were shaken by the experience on board the *Waitemata*. Baxter later said: 'They were evidently prepared to go to greater lengths against us than most of us had thought in those early days before we fully realised what we were up against.'

It was just a taste of what was to come. In Britain, France and Belgium the Allied authorities threw punishment after punishment at the men to make them relent: imprisonment, starvation, tortuous drills, beatings and Field Punishment No. 1 (the official name for the 'crucifixion'). In the end those who held out were forced up to the front lines.

All but Briggs and Baxter eventually succumbed to the intense pressure and agreed to serve, mostly in non-combatant positions. William Little, who had been locked up in the notorious Dunkirk Military Prison on arrival in England, was killed by enemy fire in September 1918, just seventeen days after agreeing to serve as a stretcher-bearer.

Baxter and Briggs refused to do even non-combatant service, because doing so would free up another man to fight, and possibly lose his life.

Baxter's existence became a battle to stay alive. He did manage to avoid further field punishment, thanks to the intervention of a New Zealand sergeant. The horrified man had come upon him and Lawrence Kirwan lashed to poles in the snow and had reprimanded the military police.

'I never saw such a damned thing done in all my life,' he'd said. 'I don't care who they are or what they've done. It's what you're doing to them I'm concerned about. I didn't think men would do such a thing.'

Within days of that last field punishment Baxter was sent up to the front. Before he left he wrote to his parents. The letter read, in part: 'As far as military service goes, I am of the same mind as ever.

It is impossible for me to serve in the army. I would a thousand times rather be put to death . . . I have suffered to the limit of my endurance, but I will never in my sane senses surrender to the evil power that has fixed its roots like a cancer on the world.'

Up at the front Baxter and Briggs were reunited. It was shortly afterwards that Briggs was dragged up to the front line. As Briggs lay in the hut recovering, the guard who was overseeing their punishment, Sergeant Booth, told Baxter that his friend wasn't expected to live and if he did he'd be shot. 'That's the way you'll be tomorrow,' Booth said.

The sergeant had a different plan for Baxter. In the morning he gave Baxter an order. Baxter refused it. It was the usual routine. Baxter had become accustomed to the beatings, and to the starvation diet Booth had imposed.

Booth struck him on the mouth and repeated the order. Again Baxter refused and again Booth punched him, making his mouth bleed. Booth kept saying, 'Do it! Do it!' Baxter kept saying, 'No!' Each time he said it Booth struck him. Soldiers who were working nearby yelled angrily at Booth, telling him to leave Baxter alone. So Booth took him out of sight.

'He began again,' wrote Baxter in his autobiography, 'this time punching me in the ribs, hard punches delivered in rapid succession, very many in the same place. The effect of this, besides being extremely painful, was irritating to the last degree. The desire to strike back was difficult to withstand. But I had made up my mind to stand it without retaliation, and stand it I did. I regarded it as part of the violence which the New Zealand Government had issued instructions to use against me. At last Booth desisted, tired out.'

Booth then asked an officer if there was any place nearby that was being heavily shelled. The man pointed out an ammunition dump that the Germans were targeting at 20-minute intervals. Booth marched Baxter to it and left him there.

'As he hurried away,' wrote Baxter, 'he called back, "I hope a shell gets you and blows you to your Maker." I stood waiting . . . Suddenly firing began again and the shells came thick and fast. I was in the midst of a storm of spouting, belching mud and fire and flying fragments. The shells seemed to strike everywhere but where I was . . . I stood and waited for what seemed inevitable death.'

Death did not come, and from that moment Booth washed his hands of him. For a brief time the pressure eased and Baxter was allowed to eat with the soldiers. But when he and the troops began the journey to the Somme, he endured another vicious beating, this time from a Captain Stevenson, and was once again denied food. At first he would hunt in tins for odd scraps and the dregs of tea but eventually he stopped feeling the hunger. Sympathetic soldiers would fill his pockets with cigarettes. 'They did not know I was getting no food,' wrote Baxter, 'and I did not wish to tell them as their rations were little enough.'

He grew gradually weaker. In one last bid for food he joined a rations line one morning and held out his tin. It was in vain.

'I turned away and lay down exhausted on the sodden earth. My head and limbs were burning and I could neither rest nor sleep. My brain was working at lightning speed but the thoughts were confused and incoherent . . . Then everything was a blank until a time, later in the morning, when I looked round me and could not see a human soul.'

He got up and staggered on until his legs could no longer carry him. So he crawled, until he came to a shell hole filled with water. He didn't have the strength to go around it. He lay down, semi-conscious, until two English soldiers came upon him and carried him to a dressing station.

In April 1918, Baxter was declared to be insane by a British medical board. He was probably suffering post-traumatic stress disorder but was far better off than most of his fellow patients.

It might have been an attempt by the British to save him from a court martial and possible execution by the New Zealand military authorities. After several months in British hospitals he was finally sent home in August 1918.

Briggs returned to New Zealand several months later. His darkest moment–being dragged to the front lines–was also his last big challenge. He eventually received medical treatment for the horrific wounds inflicted on him at Ypres and after he recovered the authorities all but gave up on their attempts to convert him. In June 1918 he was judged to be unfit for active service because of muscular rheumatism and he was invalided back to New Zealand in 1919.

Even when they returned, Baxter and Briggs weren't let off the hook. Sympathetic parliamentarian–and inaugural leader of the Labour Party–Harry Holland later relayed Briggs' post-war experience: 'They had taken him to the brink of hell and to the borderland of death, and he had not given in. When he came back he refused to take either military pay or a discharge because he said he had never been a soldier and didn't need them. Then they put him under open arrest for refusing a discharge from the Army to which he had never belonged.'

Briggs returned to his successful auctioneering and furniture business in Palmerston North. In 1936 he was elected to parliament, later to become the sole parliamentarian to vote against conscription in World War II. He died in 1960 at the age of 80.

Baxter returned to farming in Brighton and had two sons. One, Terence Baxter, became a conscientious objector in World War II. The other, James K. Baxter, became one of New Zealand's greatest poets, who wrote bitter poems protesting the Vietnam War.

In 1939 Archibald Baxter published a memoir of his wartime experience, *We Will Not Cease.* As soon as the book arrived he sent a copy to Briggs with the inscription: 'In memory of days we can't afford to forget.'

Baxter died in 1970, aged 88.

Historian David Grant, who wrote a book about the experiences of conscientious objectors in New Zealand, called their treatment in World War II 'the most astonishing recorded instance of state-sanctioned cruelty which New Zealanders have ever inflicted on fellow New Zealanders'.

Baxter and Briggs, he said, displayed immense personal and moral courage and uncompromising conviction in the face of overwhelming odds. He also acknowledged the bravery of the many ordinary soldiers who stood up for them as they were being persecuted.

Grant paid tribute to Baxter's humility—his 'saint-like absence of rancour and readiness to find humanity in the common soldier'. In 1919 Harry Holland said of Briggs: 'He was one of the best citizens that this country ever possessed. It was all very well for some members to cry "shirkers" every time one of these men was mentioned but it required more courage to do what Briggs did than it required even to go into the trenches and fight.'

Garfield Todd

Leader with a conscience

Invercargill is an unlikely hometown for an African leader and statesman but there was very little about Garfield Todd's life that was predictable. Perhaps it was his humble beginnings as a Scottish brickmaker's son in Southland, combined with his strong Christian beliefs, that set Todd on the path of becoming the conscience of a country.

In 1934, aged just 26, Todd arrived at a Christian mission in Southern Rhodesia, now Zimbabwe, with his wife Grace. He was a graduate of Otago University and the Glen Leith Bible College in Dunedin and an ordained minister in the Church of Christ.

The couple immediately dived in to setting up a school for African children at their mission in Dadaya. It was the start of a lifetime of devotion to the country. It was also their first taste of politics, though they didn't know it–one of their young primary teachers was the country's future dictator, Robert Mugabe. Many years later Mugabe would turn against them.

Todd and his wife fell in love with the country and they bought a large tract of land near Dadaya to establish a farm. They named it 'Hokonui Ranch', after the range of hills in his native Southland.

At that time Southern Rhodesia was ruled by a minority government dominated by a white colonial elite. The ruling classes viewed missionaries with suspicion on account of their liberal ideas. They became so unpopular that when Todd's ten-year-old daughter

Judith was asked what her father did for a living, she would reply, 'He's a New Zealander.'

Despite his commitment to his religion, it was Todd's success as a farmer that brought him into the political swirl of the country. It is perhaps surprising that a man whose life revolved around trying to improve the lot of local Africans through education, religion and medical care should become involved with a colonial regime that was inherently racist, but he saw that as the only way to bring about effective change was from inside the political system.

In 1946, Todd stood for the United Rhodesia Party in his local Shabani seat and won. He became an energetic parliamentarian, and the church minister from New Zealand soon became a government minister in Africa. His rise through the ranks was rapid—in 1953 he was elected prime minister of Southern Rhodesia.

Over the next four years, Todd introduced a variety of measures to improve the living and working conditions of native Africans in the country. He paved the way for every child to receive primary education and changed the law so that black Africans were able to join trade unions.

Though the changes were positive, they were minor compared with the massive moves towards independence and majority rule that were afoot in other African countries.

When Todd came to power, a mere two per cent of black Rhodesians qualified to vote. In 1957, he proposed changes to voting eligibility using educational qualifications to increase that number to 16 per cent. Though it was an improvement, it was hardly radical. But it was deeply unpopular in white colonial circles.

Todd's entire cabinet resigned in protest in January 1958 and he was eventually dumped as party leader. In his farewell address, Todd made it clear that the political overhaul hadn't dulled his desire for equality in the country. 'We must make it possible for every individual to lead the good life, to win a place in the sun,' he said.

'We are in danger of becoming a race of fear-ridden neurotics—we who live in the finest country on Earth.'

Having suffered such a humiliating defeat, Todd could easily have faded into the background and focused on running his farm. But that wasn't his style. He couldn't sit back and watch his adopted country slide even further into white minority rule, with blacks being little more than slaves in their own country. Todd found his voice was welcomed at the United Nations, a forum that he addressed several times, speaking out against colonialism in Africa. He believed firmly that Southern Rhodesia should not gain independence from Britain before majority rule was in place, and he missed no opportunity to speak out in the media.

When the right wing politician Ian Smith came to power in 1964, he made no secret of his distaste for the increasingly radical views of his predecessor. Smith saw Todd as such a threat that on 18 October 1965 he ordered the Kiwi missionary and his wife to be placed under house arrest. Smith's plan was to intimidate and silence his biggest critic while he declared Southern Rhodesia's unilateral independence, changing the country's name to Rhodesia and installing a conservative right-wing white government.

The couple's incarceration lasted a year but didn't quell Garfield's desire for majority rule in the country. He lobbied the international community, focusing on the country's former colonial masters in Britain, and advocated international sanctions against Rhodesia. In January 1972, Garfield Todd and his equally outspoken daughter Judith were arrested and spent a month in jail. They were returned to Hokonui under house arrest. Judith went into exile but Garfield would not leave the country he'd become devoted to. Despite international condemnation of Smith's treatment of Todd, the elder statesman was banned from writing or receiving letters and his phone line was often cut.

This remained the status quo until 1976, when the Todds were released from house arrest following a vigorous international campaign for them to be freed. By then the writing was on the wall for Smith's racist regime. A guerrilla war for independence, led in part by Robert Mugabe, was well underway in Rhodesia. Despite the turmoil this war brought to the country, the Todds remained at Hokonui and continued to speak out against the Smith regime.

It wasn't until 1979 that Smith and his cronies realised their game was up. They surrendered leadership of Rhodesia on 12 December. With independence came full African suffrage. Elections were held under international supervision in 1980. Robert Mugabe's Zanu-PF party came to power and renamed the country Zimbabwe. Garfield Todd was appointed as a senator in the first parliament of the newly independent country.

In 1985, the 77-year-old stood down from the senate. The following year he received a knighthood from his native New Zealand. Far from retiring, Todd found himself thrown back into the political arena as Robert Mugabe's regime became increasingly violent and anti-white. He was outspoken in his criticism of his former student. Persecution followed.

There was no more poignant sign of just how far the pendulum had swung away from Todd's dream for 'every individual to lead the good life, to win a place in the sun', than when he was stripped of his right to vote in the 2002 election because he refused to give up his dual New Zealand/Zimbabwean nationality. He was quoted as saying, 'Just as we stood with courage against the racism of the past, so today we must stand with courage against the terror of the present. Come what may, I will be going to the polling station to claim my right as a very senior citizen of Zimbabwe, to cast my ballot for good against evil.'

He turned up to vote, but was turned away by a polling agent who was a former student from Dadya mission school. Within months he was dead, at age 94.

His Christian faith meant that he always forgave those who persecuted him. He once said his philosophy of life was, 'Just keep throwing your bread upon the waters; if you're lucky, it will come back as ham sandwiches.'

Whina Cooper

Woman of mana

Whina Cooper was getting tired. Arthritis was leaching the strength from her joints and causing her great pain. She could walk only short distances, and then only with assistance. It was 1974 and she was 79.

'My life is over,' she told a journalist from the *Auckland Star*. 'All I can do now is talk.'

It was 61 years since she'd made her first stand on behalf of Maori. When she was a teenager her community at Whakarapa on the Hokianga Harbour had become angry when a farmer had begun to drain a 20-hectare area of mudflats for conversion to farming. The man, Bob Holland, had acquired a lease from the Marine Department, but Cooper's people fished and collected shellfish in the estuary, and raced their horses on it in the dry summer months.

Her father, Heremia Te Wake, a respected elder and businessman, began to lobby for a political solution but was concerned that by the time a call was made the mudflats would be pasture.

At a meeting of the local Maori, Cooper (then Whina Te Wake) was asked for her opinion. Although she was just eighteen, she was astute and confident and was considered to understand the Pakeha system. She suggested that while her father pursued diplomatic solutions, the younger people of the community would simply fill in the drains as the farmer dug them—ostensibly on their own initiative so her father could not be blamed. The rest of the meeting was spent arranging the collection of spades and shovels.

When Holland turned up for work the next morning he was bewildered to discover that his trenches had disappeared. As he and his sons started digging, Cooper's team of young men and women appeared and began calmly shovelling the sand and mud back into the trenches. The farmer shouted threats at them, argued with them, pleaded with them. They listened courteously but refused to answer, and refused to leave. They remained calm and congenial—Cooper was adamant it was to be a peaceful protest, not a confrontation.

The following day Holland and his sons rose earlier. By the time Cooper and her shovel squad arrived they'd dug 50 metres of trenches. The squad set to work filling them in again. The farmer left and reported the act to the police. About 20 of the group were fined for trespassing but, crucially, Holland didn't try digging again. In the meantime their local MP, Peter Buck, had managed to persuade the Marine Department to cancel Holland's lease. He was paid compensation and the mudflats survived.

Shortly after her *Auckland Star* interview Cooper was made a Commander of the British Empire (CBE)—one step down from a dame. Her biographer, Michael King, later noted: 'This was seen by the press as the crowning and final touch to a life of service.'

In fact her most memorable act was yet to come. She had a dream around that time that she went to heaven and met God. She recalled: 'He was only a short chap with a Pakeha face and a long beard, and he had these eyes that flashed and flickered. I could hardly look at Him. Anyway, he said to me in Maori, "Where are you going?" And I said, "I'm coming up here, to Heaven." He said, "Oh no you're not. Not yet. Your work's not completed." After that I thought, oh well, I'll just have to keep going.'

It wasn't long before the veteran campaigner for Maori answered another rallying cry. It was on the same theme as that first cause that had prompted her to pick up a spade: land. In 1975 she was approached by a group of young urban radicals who were setting up a campaign to combat further loss of Maori land and needed a leader. She accepted, and declared that it would be the last and most important campaign of her life.

Cooper calculated that just three per cent of New Zealand's land was in Maori ownership, almost half what it had been ten years earlier. And the erosion was continuing, under the auspices of half a dozen acts of parliament. To draw Pakeha attention to the issue, Cooper proposed a hikoi, or march. And not just any march: she suggest a dignified protest walk from Te Hapua, a tiny settlement near the tip of the North Island, to Wellington. The marchers would stop at marae along the route to discuss their grievances. Cooper asked for nominations for a man to lead the hikoi but the group insisted that the honour should fall to her.

In the months that followed, Whina travelled around the country to galvanise support. It was not unanimous. A Ngatiwai elder, Waipu Pita, feared that Cooper and her march would discredit Matiu Rata, the minister of Maori affairs in the Labour government. 'We lower our race when we adopt such tactics . . . for when Maoris march, it is to war, and trouble is what I fear from this march.'

Rata too was concerned; he regarded the existence of Cooper's group, Te Ropu o te Matakite, as a vote of no confidence in him. He issued a press statement that said there was no need for the march, as tens of thousands of acres of land were already being given back.

Matakite pointed out that the land being 'given back' was already in Maori ownership. They countered with their own press statement that explained the march was an illustration of bitterness that the government had not done more, and they hoped to convince parliament to act with greater haste. 'It is also designed to provide the minister with the support to implement more meaningful policies. Despite government action, we continue to lose Maori land.'

Rata's secretary even threatened to close all the marae along the route. Cooper replied, 'That's all right, as long as the road isn't shut we'll sleep there.'

Cooper came in for personal attacks. A rumour began that she had sold family land in Northland to Pakeha at great profit. She confronted one of her critics at the Department of Maori Affairs and he apologised and admitted the allegations were false.

After months of planning, placating and fundraising, Cooper led the first marchers out of the Te Hapua Marae at 9.30 a.m. on 14 September 1975. A few months shy of her eightieth birthday, she was too frail to walk long distances, so she planned to travel much of the way in a car behind the procession. About 50 people were determined to cover the entire 1100 kilometres on foot.

As they left the marae, a *New Zealand Herald* photographer snapped a picture of Cooper leading the procession out of the marae, hand in hand with her three-year-old granddaughter. A dirt road wound into the distance ahead of them. It was published prominently in the newspaper and immediately people started taking notice.

The march took 30 days. They spent each night at a different marae, usually debating at length their actions and objectives. Night after night Cooper would take a leading role in discussions. King called it 'an extraordinary display of stamina for a person of her age'.

On the roads, the reception was mixed. There was plenty of support. Strangers would bring them food and drink and cars tooted in support. As they neared Auckland, the harbour board gave them permission to walk over the Auckland Harbour Bridge. It was a triumphant crossing.

But there was ugliness. They received anonymous threats and some bystanders were loudly rude. In Wellington someone spread broken shells along their route, presumably knowing that some of the marchers were barefoot.

It was a tribute to the strength of Cooper's leadership that the marchers remained patient and peaceful in the face of such hostility.

By the time they reached parliament on 13 October they were 5000 strong. They were met by Prime Minister Bill Rowling, who told them their march was not in vain, and the government would continue its efforts to ensure absolute equity for Maori.

King noted that the long-term outcome of the march was less decisive. 'The conduct of the march itself, however, had been an eloquent tribute to Whina's energy and mana and a potent symbol of the Maori cultural renaissance which gathered momentum in the years that followed.'

In between the mudflats protest and the land march came six decades of hard work: as a leader in the Northland community and in Auckland; as the founding president of the Maori Women's Welfare League; as a community worker; as a government advisor; as a regular commentator in the media; as a mother of seven; as a fundraiser for the war effort in the 1940s; as a campaigner for Maori housing, education, health and social needs; as a public speaker; even as a rugby coach.

Throughout her life, Cooper faced disapproval from her own people: for marrying her first husband in secret, and taking up with her second while still with him; for her tendency to embark on projects and campaigns without waiting for consensus from elders and colleagues; for her outspoken nature. Sometimes the criticism stung, but it probably also strengthened her resolve and her armour.

Cooper died in 1994. Her funeral was attended by thousands of people and broadcast live on television. Before she died her CBE was upgraded to a DBE, making her a dame, and she became a member of the Order of New Zealand.

'If some can get to these heights, we all can,' she once said. 'There is no excuse for people saying we have to go to university to be able to do things. I came out of the tea tree, out of a nikau hut, out of the country. With the work that you do for people, and in helping them, you can rise.'

Ken Gray
Graham Mourie
Bruce Robertson
Trevor Richards

Standing up against racism

It was 17 November 1980 and renowned All Black captain Graham Mourie was afraid. It was a very different sensation from the nerves he felt before a rugby test. He was afraid of betraying a sport that had been good to him. He was afraid of standing alone.

He pulled out a notebook that served as a diary and wrote: 'Today I announced that I would not play against South Africa.'

It was a big call. Mourie knew that it could spell the end of his captaincy. It could even be the end of his All Black career. But he was convinced it was the right thing to do.

He wasn't the first All Black to make a stand against South's Africa's apartheid policy, under which black and coloured players were banned from its national rugby team, the Springboks. More than ten years earlier, legendary All Black prop Ken Gray had retired early from the game rather than join the 1970 tour to South Africa. He believed it wasn't right to play against a racially selected team. Though Maori and Samoan players were named in the All Black touring squad, they were only allowed to tour because the South

African authorities declared them 'honorary whites'. Like many New Zealanders, Gray was disgusted.

He didn't immediately go public with the reasons for his retirement. He timed the announcement for Christmas 1969 in the hope of a quiet exit. Though he was confident in his beliefs, they were at odds with the prevailing view in New Zealand rugby that South Africa's politics were irrelevant to its sporting ties, and he wasn't ready to come under public scrutiny. But eventually the truth came out.

'My announcement was seen by many as a betrayal,' said Gray later. 'Rugby players felt undermined.'

Apartheid had been entrenched in South Africa since 1950. By the early 1970s international pressure on the country was intensifying. Gray was then back on his Plimmerton farm and Mourie was studying law at Victoria University. He was also playing his way up the rugby ranks, dreaming of becoming an All Black. While some of his student friends were starting to take sides on the Springbok rugby debate, Mourie remained an interested but silent observer.

In 1972, with an election looming and a Springbok tour of New Zealand scheduled for the following year, things got political. It's an indication of how important the All Black/Springbok rivalry was to New Zealand that it became the subject of election promises in two successive campaigns. That year Labour leader Norman Kirk promised that he would allow the tour, despite the international condemnation of apartheid.

South Africa was then considered New Zealand's greatest rugby rival, and the All Blacks looked upon a test match against the Boks as the apex of their careers. However, the sides rarely met. Tours came around only once or twice a decade, and were phenomenally popular in both countries.

But public sentiment in New Zealand was growing against apartheid. Once in office, Kirk backtracked on his vow, recognising that the potential for mass protest presented the possibility of the 'greatest eruption of violence this country has ever known'. In April 1973 he cancelled the tour.

His political rival, Robert Muldoon, was quick to get mileage out of it. He recognised that it was a vote-changing issue, and promised to reinstate tours. He was elected in 1975 and immediately instituted a policy of no political interference in sport.

Mourie was still undecided on the issue in 1976 when it was announced that the All Blacks would tour South Africa. And fate ensured he wasn't forced to make a call—a rib injury kept him away from the trials that would decide the touring squad. He later reflected that he probably would have gone.

'At that stage in my career, any purer motives of morality, responsibility to my country and the greater game of rugby were quickly sublimated by the desire to be an All Black,' he wrote in his 1982 autobiography.

As the All Blacks' date of departure drew near, thousands of anti-tour protesters marched in Auckland, Wellington and Christchurch, under the banner of the protest movement HART (Halt All Racist Tours). The United Nations Special Committee Against Apartheid called for the New Zealand government and the New Zealand Rugby Football Union (NZRFU) to call off the tour. The Australian government announced it would refuse to allow the All Blacks' plane to refuel in its territory, so a circuitous route was mapped out.

Days before the All Blacks were due to leave, reports starting coming in about riots in a South African city called Soweto. On the morning of 16 June, 30,000 schoolchildren had begun a peaceful demonstration at a secondary school against the enforced teaching of Afrikaans, when police arrived and opened fire. The South African government admitted to 25 deaths and 200 injuries but news reports put the death toll at nearer 500. A national uprising began.

Despite this, on 22 June the All Blacks flew out as scheduled. New Zealand lost more than just the series. They lost the respect of much of the world—later that year 28 countries boycotted the Olympics in protest at New Zealand's sporting links with South Africa.

One of the touring team, centre Bruce Robertson found apartheid abhorrent, both in sport and in South African society. He was also bitter about a spot of dodgy refereeing that saw him denied two test tries.

Ken Gray told writer David McGill in 1977 that it wasn't Soweto and apartheid that had eventually turned New Zealand against South Africa. 'It was that dirty third test. "Dirty South African bastards," people said. "We should never have gone there."'

Mourie followed the tour from home. He later wrote: 'It was gradually becoming clear that the situation in South Africa and its ramifications for New Zealand and rugby were decidedly not to my liking.'

On 18 September 1976 Mourie, then aged 24, was not only picked for the All Blacks, he was named captain. Even he was surprised.

To his relief, it looked like he would not be forced to make a call on playing South Africa. In June 1977 the Commonwealth declared that it had an 'urgent duty' to combat 'the evil of apartheid' by discouraging sporting contact with South Africa. New Zealand was a signatory to the agreement. Mourie was confident it meant there would be no further significant sports contact between the countries, and the planned 1981 Springbok tour wouldn't go ahead.

But by late 1980 Muldoon had reverted to his 'no politics in sport' line and the NZRFU ploughed ahead with plans for the tour. For Mourie it became a question of conscience. He informed All Blacks managers he would not be available for selection.

In that journal entry of 17 November 1980, Mourie was plagued by doubts: 'This week has been the most miserable, difficult, solitary week in my life. A week of pressure from the media, of pressure from within myself . . . I'm tired and my mind is working overtime. A veritable civil war, a bloodless insurrection of my sense of loyalty against my conscience. And occasionally pulsing in the back of my mind, a dominant thought. Be strong.'

His decision made a big splash in the media, in New Zealand and overseas. The reaction from his team mates and managers and the public was mixed. Some sympathised, some ignored him, some tried to talk him round, a few were abusive. Like Ken Gray, Mourie played down the abuse, but both received hate mail. It was fortunate they were each so physically intimidating.

Prominent Anglican Bishop Godfrey Wilson praised Mourie's decision to let what he believed to be morally right take precedence over personal ambition and pleasure.

'Suddenly, from the rugby man of the moment, the man at the very peak of form and fame, comes this quiet, firm voice: "I think there's a moral issue. And it's so important that . . . I can't play against the Springboks."'

Five days after Mourie's announcement, the disillusioned Robertson also declared he would refuse to play on moral grounds. 'I could see things happening to rugby which weren't good for the game, and I wanted to get out of it,' the centre explained later. He is said to have lost interest in rugby after that, at least for a time. It marked the end of what had been a glittering All Black career.

On 19 July 1981 the Springboks arrived. While Mourie and Robertson kept their heads down, Gray had by then become a public face in the anti-apartheid movement. The groups HART and CARE (Citizens Association for Racial Equality) mobilised thousands of people to protest against the tour as it moved through the country. One of their favourite chants was: 'Two, four, six, eight, Graham Mourie is our mate.'

In Hamilton, protesters charged onto the field before a test match and managed to get the game cancelled. But there were consequences. They were dealt with violently by baton-wielding riot police and many were badly beaten by rugby fans. It was Stalinesque.

Among the protesters outside one of the games stood a towering farmer from Plimmerton. It was almost inconceivable that a legendary All Black would try to disrupt an All Black game, and in doing so Gray further alienated many of his former rugby friends.

'I make no apologies for the way I feel,' he said. 'My only regret is that I didn't confess my feelings about South Africa when I announced my retirement.'

Thousands of New Zealanders risked their reputations, liberty and bodies to stand against apartheid in 1981. More than 1500 were arrested in what became the largest police operation in New Zealand history. War hero Charles Upham condemned the tour. Cartoonist Murray Ball joined the protests. Trade unionist Sonja Davies took a punch in the stomach from one rugby fan and was spat on by another—a young Maori man. Future mayor Tim Shadbolt was arrested. Some genuinely feared they would die.

HART co-founder Trevor Richards caught perhaps the most flak of any one person. Richards was a pioneer in New Zealand's anti-apartheid movement and a good-humoured advocate of peaceful protest. By 1981 he'd been active in the cause for twelve years so he'd become accustomed to being knocked around, verbally and physically. The satirist Tom Scott had once told him he would one day become New Zealand's first political martyr. Even so, he was taken aback by the vitriol in some of the attacks on him.

In 1978 the chair of parliament's foreign affairs select committee, R.L.G. Talbot, stood up in parliament and accused Richards of being 'a traitor to the western world, a traitor to New Zealand, and a traitor to the Commonwealth'. He lamented that New Zealand didn't have a law to control 'people like Richards'. Muldoon was quoted saying much the same thing on several occasions and, Richards later discovered, had asked Crown Law if he could be prosecuted under the laws relating to sedition and treason, and—bizarrely—race relations. Presumably, the answer was 'no'.

In 1977 a drunk New Zealand man in his fifties spotted Richards on a plane as he returned from a trip to Africa for HART. He pulled Richards up by his hair and started shouting, 'Traitor! This man is a traitor.' He kept up a tirade of verbal abuse until a flight attendant ordered him to his seat.

As the 1981 tour drew near, Richards braced for a renewed onslaught. One rugby fan rang him in the middle of the night a month before the tour, threatening to blow his brains out. A few minutes later he rang back to add, 'And I'm going to blow your f****** house up.' A few weeks later a brick came crashing through his lounge window, but his head and house remained intact.

Somehow Richards managed to survive the protests without serious injury. But there was one last surprise in store. In mid-September, shortly after the tour ended, he was walking past the Carlton Hotel in Willis Street, Wellington, when a stocky, middle-aged man stumbled out.

He took one look at Richards and, according to journalist Geoff Chapple: 'Richards glimpsed the face of old New Zealand just before the man pulled back and hit him, as hard as he was able, in the head.'

Apart from disrupting the Hamilton game, the protesters had been unsuccessful in stopping the tour. Their efforts proved more fruitful in the long term. An All Black tour to South Africa in 1985 was stopped by the High Court (though a 'rebel tour' went ahead the following year), and the All Blacks and Springboks didn't meet again until South Africa began to dismantle apartheid in the early 1990s.

A HART organiser, John Minto, later said: 'As a result of the protests here, no other major rugby-playing country would accept the Springboks until apartheid was gone. We closed down South African rugby for ten years.'

In 1994 the Springboks finally returned to New Zealand. Richards was bemused when invitations poured in from rugby and political circles to receptions, functions and games. At a Wellington function, he recalled, 'Politicians who previously could not mention my name without choking were all smiles . . . I had very pleasant chats with Springboks captain Francois Pienaar, the South African ambassador, the chairman of the NZRFU and [Prime Minister] Jim Bolger. It was all a bit freaky.'

The following year, when South African political prisoner turned president Nelson Mandela visited New Zealand, he told Governor-General Catherine Tizard that he had heard the news of the Hamilton protest from prison. 'It felt like the sun coming out,' he said.

Despite grumbles from some sections of the rugby community, Mourie resumed his captaincy of the All Blacks just months after the 1981 tour. He later said he was disappointed he never got to play the Springboks, but didn't regret his decision.

'I felt that playing would have given tacit support to the unjust regime in South Africa–it would have been hypocritical of me to say apartheid was wrong but go ahead and play just because I wanted to.'

Acknowledgements

Many thanks to Nicola McCloy and Christine Sheehy for your heroic efforts. Thanks to Brad, Oscar and Leo McEvoy for all your support. And kudos to the rest of the great team at Allen & Unwin: Melanie Laville Moore, Lucie L'Estrange, Abba Renshaw, Josie Brennan, Neil Brown, Ross Lorimer and Jennie Goodman. Thanks also to Janet Hunt and Nick Turzynski for their design work.

Bibliography

Books

Apiata, Willie and Little, Paul, *Willie Apiata VC—the reluctant hero*, Penguin, Auckland, 2008

Alexander, Caroline, *The Endurance*, Bloomsbury, London, 1998

Anderton, Jim, *Unsung Heroes—portraits of inspiring New Zealanders*, Random House, Auckland, 1999

Baxter, Archibald, *We Will Not Cease*, Cape Catley, Auckland, 2003 reprint

Baxter, Millicent, *The Memoirs of Millicent Baxter*, Cape Catley, Queen Charlotte Sound, 1981

BBC Worldwide, *Low! The Twentieth Century's Greatest Cartoonist*, BBC History Magazines, London, 2002

Bell, Terry, *Hillary of Everest: the Years After*, Wilson & Horton, Auckland, 1973

Booth, Pat, *Edmund Hillary: the Life of a Legend*, Moa Beckett, Auckland, 1993

Braddon, Russell, *Nancy Wake: SOE's Greatest Heroine*, Sutton Publishing, Gloucestershire, 2005 (first published by Cassell in 1956)

Brockie, Bob (ed), *The Penguin Eyewitness History of New Zealand*, Penguin, Auckland, 2002

Bryder, Linda, *A History of the 'Unfortunate Experiment' at National Women's Hospital*, Auckland University Press, Auckland, 2009

Buick, T, *The Rebellion of Hone Heke*, Government Print, Wellington, 1926

Bunkle, Phillida, *Second Opinion: The politics of women's health in New Zealand*, Oxford University Press, Auckland, 1988

Butler, Mark, *Fred Hollows: leaving the world a better place*, Cardigan Street Publishers, Victoria, 1995

Chapple, Geoff, *1981: The Tour*, Reed, Wellington, 1984

Church, Olive and Zajas, Jay, *Applying telecommunications and technology from a global business perspective*, Haworth Press, New York, 1997

Coney, Sandra, *The Unfortunate Experiment*, Penguin, Auckland, 1988

Coney, Sandra (ed), *Unfinished Business: What Happened to the Cartwright Report?* Women's Health Action, Auckland, 1993

Conly, Geoff and Stewart, Graham, *New Zealand Tragedies on the Track*, Grantham House, Wellington, 1991 (first published 1986)

Cowan, James, *Hero Stories of New Zealand*, Harry H Tombs, Wellington, 1935

Cowan, James, *The New Zealand Wars: A History of the Maori Campaigns and the Pioneering Period*, R.E. Owen, Wellington, 1956

Cox, Geoffrey, *Eyewitness: a memoir of Europe in the 1930s*, University of Otago Press, Dunedin, 1999.

Crawford, John (ed), *No Better Death: the Great War diaries and letters of William G Malone*, Reed, Auckland, 2005

Davin, D. M., *Crete*, Historical Publications Branch, Wellington, 1953

Derby, Mark (ed), *Kiwi Companeros: New Zealand and the Spanish Civil War*, Canterbury University Press, Christchurch, 2009

Devaliant, Judith, *Kate Sheppard: The fight for women's votes in New Zealand*, Penguin, Auckland, 1992

Fiske, Pat and Johnson, Michael, *Memories of Fred*, ABC Books, Sydney, 1995

Fitzsimons, Peter, *Nancy Wake: the inspiring story of one of the war's greatest heroines*, Harper Collins, London, 2002

Glue, W. A. and Pringle, D. J. C., *20 Battalion and Armoured Regiment*, Historical Publications Branch, Wellington, 1957

Grant, David, *Field Punishment No. 1: Archibald Baxter, Mark Briggs & New Zealand's anti-militarist tradition*, Steele Roberts Publishers, Wellington, 2008

Gustafson, Barry, *His Way: A Biography of Robert Muldoon*, Auckland University Press, Auckland, 2000

Hall-Jones, John, *Pioneers of Te Anau*, Craig Printing, Invercargill, 1984

Hill, S. & J. Hill, *Richard Henry of Resolution Island,* John McIndoe, Dunedin, 1987

Hillary, Edmund, *Nothing Venture, Nothing Win*, Hodder & Stoughton, London, 1975

Hillary, Edmund, *Schoolhouse in the Clouds*, Hodder & Stoughton, London, 1964

Hillary, Edmund, *View from the Summit*, Doubleday, London, 1999

Hobbs, Mary, *Kiwi Tucker for the Soul*, New Zealand Outside, Christchurch, 2000

Holland, Harry, *Armageddon or Calvary: the conscientious objectors of New Zealand and the process of their conversion*, The Maoriland Worker Printing and Publishing Company, Wellington, 1919

Hollows, Fred and Corris, Peter, *Fred Hollows: an autobiography*, Kerr Publishing, Sydney, 1992

Howitt, Bob, *New Zealand Rugby Greats*, Hodder Moa Beckett, Auckland, 1997

Johnston, Alexa, *Sir Edmund Hillary: an extraordinary life*, Penguin, Auckland, 2005

Kennedy, Royd, *Firefighter: An Autobiography*, Cape Catley Ltd, Whatamango Bay, Queen Charlotte Sound, 1997

King, Michael, *Whina: A Biography of Whina Cooper*, Penguin, Auckland, 1983

Lambert, Max and Hartley, Jim, *The Wahine Disaster*, A.H. & A.W. Reed, Wellington, 1969

Lange, David, *My Life*, Penguin, Auckland, 2005

Lange, David, *Nuclear Free–the New Zealand way*, Penguin, Auckland, 1990

Lansing, Alfred, *Endurance*, Weidenfeld & Nicolson, London, 2000

Low, David, *Low's Autobiography*, Michael Joseph, London, 1956

Low, David, *Years of Wrath: a Cartoon History 1932–1945*, Victor Gollancz, London, 1986 (first published 1949)

McCallum, Janet, *Women in the House*, Cape Catley, Auckland, 1993

MacDonald, C (ed), *The Vote, the Pill and the Demon Drink*, Bridget Williams Books, Wellington, 1993

McFarlene Stuart, *The Erebus Papers*, Avon Press Ltd, Auckland, 1991

McGill, David, *Good Old Kiwi Identities*, Grantham House, Wellington, 2000

McGregor Dunnett, Harding, *Shackleton's Boat*, Neville & Harding, Kent, 1996

McKinnon, Malcolm, *Independence and Foreign Policy: New Zealand in the World since 1935*, Auckland University Press, Auckland, 1993

McLintock, Alexander (ed), *Te Ara: the Encylopaedia of New Zealand*, Government Printer, Wellington, 1966

Mahon Peter, *Verdict on Erebus*, William Collins Publishers Ltd, 1984

Mahon Sam, *My Father's Shadow: A Portrait of Justice Peter Mahon*, Longacre Press, Dunedin 2008

Makarios, Emmanuel, *The Wahine Disaster–A Tragedy Remembered*, Grantham House, Wellington, 2003

Manning, Joanna, *The Cartwright Papers*, Bridget Williams Books, Wellington, 2009

Matheson, Clare, *Fate Cries Enough*, Sceptre, Auckland, 1989

Mourie, Graham, *Graham Mourie: Captain*, Moa Publications, Auckland, 1982

O'Connor, Martin, *The New Zealand European Connection*, Grantham House, Wellington, 1989

Orange, Claudia (ed), *Dictionary of New Zealand Biography*, five volumes, Department of Internal Affairs, Wellington, 1990–2000

Orange, Vincent, *Sir Keith Park*, Methuen, London, 1984

Phillips, J, Boyack, N and Malone, EP (eds), *The Great Adventure: New Zealand soldiers describe the First World War*, Allen and Unwin, Wellington, 1988

Pomare, Maui, *Legends of the Maori (Volume 2)*, Southern Reprints, Papakura, 1989

Richards, Trevor, *Dancing on our Bones: New Zealand, South Africa, Rugby and Racism*, Bridget Williams Books, Wellington, 1999

Romanos, Joseph, *Famous Flankers*, Rugby Press, Auckland, 1990

Russ Ramsay, Cynthia, *Sir Edmund Hillary and the People of Everest*, the Excellence Foundation, Atlanta, 2002

Sandford, Kenneth, *Mark of the Lion*, Penguin, Auckland, 1962 (2003 reprint)

Sargison, Patricia, *Notable Women in New Zealand Health*, Longman Paul, Auckland, 1993

Seymour-Ure, Colin and Schoff, Jim, *David Low*, Secker & Warburg, London, 1985

Stewart, Graham, *The Tangiwai Disaster: a Christmas Eve tragedy*, Grantham House, Wellington, 2003

Stewart, Graham, *Tangiwai Disaster and 30 other railway accidents in New Zealand*, Wilson & Horton, Auckland, 1972

Thomson, John, *Shackleton's Captain*, Hazard Press, Christchurch, 1998

Tolerton, Jane, *Ettie: A life of Ettie Rout*, Penguin, Auckland, 1992

Verdon, Paul, *Tribute: Ranking the Greatest All Blacks of All Time*, Cumulus, Auckland, 2001

Vette, Gordon, *Impact Erebus*, Hodder & Stoughton, Auckland, 1983

Wake, Nancy, *The White Mouse*, Pan Macmillan, Sydney, 1997 (2006 reprint; first published by Sun Books in 1985)

Waite, Fred, *The New Zealanders at Gallipoli*, Whitcombe and Tombs, Auckland, 1921

Waring, Marilyn, *Women, Politics and Power*, Unwin Paperbacks, Sydney, 1985

Wilson, O, From *Hongi Hika to Hone Heke*, John McIndoe, Dunedin, 1985

Worsley, Frank, *Shackleton's Boat Journey*, Pimlico, London, 1940 (1999 reprint)

Articles with author credits

Adams, Daniel, 'Rescue beat call to help in search', *Waikato Times*, 28 September 2000

Ansley, Bruce, 'Out of the Shadows', *The New Zealand Listener*, 6 September 2008

Barton, Chris. 'An unfortunate revision', *New Zealand Herald*, 15 August 2009

Beaumont, Nathan 'Blaze of Glory', *Dominion Post*, 2 May 2009

Bingham, Eugene and McFadden, Suzanne, 'Jacinta Amey', *New Zealand Herald*, 18 September 2007

Brooker, Jarrod, 'Erebus Tragedy: 30 years on', *New Zealand Herald*, 28 November 2009

Cheng, Derek and Houlahan, Mike, 'Moment that won the Cross', *New Zealand Herald*, 3 July 2007

Cleary, Greta, 'Tears as owner receives George's medal', *Taranaki Daily News*, 12 February 2009

Coney, Sandra, 'An Unfortunate History', *Metro*, October 2009

Cornwell, Rupert, 'Sir Garfield Todd, Courageous southern African statesman', *The Independent*, 14 October 2002

Cowan, James, 'Famous New Zealanders: Three Great Maori Leaders: Hongi Hika, Hone Heke, and Tamati Waka Nene', *New Zealand Railways Magazine*, 2 December 1935

Cowan, James, 'Famous New Zealanders: Te Whiti, of Taranaki: The Story of a Patriot and Peacemaker', *New Zealand Railways Magazine*, 1 October 1934

Devereux, Monique and Eames, David, 'Heroes among us: Brave New Zealanders fight forces of nature', *New Zealand Herald*, 29 January 2005

Donovan, Brooke, 'Faith, hope, love—three words summed up teacher', *New Zealand Herald*, 23 April 2008

Fickling, David, 'A belated salute for war heroine', *The Guardian*, 23 February 2004

Frankham, James, 'Great White Shark', *New Zealand Geographic*, January 2009

Gamble, Warren, 'The Herald's New Zealander of the year', *New Zealand Herald*, 21 December 2002

Garner, Theresa, 'Honours: Questions fly over belated award', *New Zealand Herald*, 23 Oct 1999

Gower, Patrick, 'A tragic force of nature', *New Zealand Herald*, 19 April 2008

Gower, Patrick and McKenzie-Minifie, Martha, 'Teacher tied himself to disabled teen in bid to save him', *New Zealand Herald*, 19 April 2008

Greenslade, Nicholas, 'Different colour, same sort of tyranny', *The New Statesman*, 14 October 2002

Gregory, Angela, 'Families remember shocking day', *New Zealand Herald*, 12 February 2008

Haines Leah, 'What the PM knew about Erebus', *New Zealand Herald*, 12 February 2008.

Hill, Ruth, 'Protests a turning point in the history of New Zealand', *New Zealand Herald*, 8 July 2006

Houlahan, Mike, 'Emotion rules day for proud and humble VC winner', *New Zealand Herald*, 27 July 2007

Hulbert, Jayne, 'Hero Jack Russell to receive Purple Heart,' *Taranaki Daily News*, 5 May 2007

Johnson, RW, 'Mugabe was rotten from the start', *The Sunday Times*, 23 September 2007

Jones, Cliff, 'Turangi Land Search and Rescue Group, Runner up in the Trustpower service to the Community award', *NZLSAR News*, 3 June 2002

Kawharu, Freda Rankin, 'Heke Pokai, Hone Wiremu ?–1850', *Dictionary of New Zealand Biography*, updated 22 June 2007, www.dnzb.govt.nz

Keatley, P, Meldrum, M, 'Sir Garfield Todd, liberal Rhodesian premier brought down over black reforms', *The Guardian*, 14 October 2002

Keenan, Danny. 'Te Whiti-o-Rongomai III, Erueti ? - 1907'. *Dictionary of New Zealand Biography*, updated 22 June 2007, www.dnzb.govt.nz

Lomas, David, 'The last rescue', *Sunday Star-Times*, 16 March 2008

Lomas, David, 'The long wait', *NZ Listener*, 29 March 2008

McKenzie-Minifie, Martha, 'Survivor's story: Taken by the river', *New Zealand Herald*, 17 April 2008

Moore, Christopher, 'A son's sketch of Peter Mahon', *The Press*, 15 August 2008

Morris, Jan, 'Edmund Hillary and Tenzing Norgay', *Time*, 14 June 1999

Ormerod, Robin. 'Henry, Richard Treacy 1845–1929', *Dictionary of New Zealand Biography*, updated 22 June 2007, www.dnzb.govt.nz

O'Rourke, Simon, 'Bravery awards: Mountain men honoured in deadly blizzard rescue', *New Zealand Herald*, 14 October 2006

Peat, Neville, 'Last, loneliest', *Heritage New Zealand*, Spring 2007

Potter, Tony, 'Saved by a reluctant hero', *Sunday Star-Times*, 1 October 2000

Pugsley, Chris. 'Malone, William George 1859–1915', *Dictionary of New Zealand Biography*, updated 22 June 2007, www.dnzb.govt.nz

Rice, Geoffrey W. 'Averill, Leslie Cecil Lloyd 1897–1981', *Dictionary of New Zealand Biography*, updated 22 June 2007, www.dnzb.govt.nz

Rowan, Juliet and Dearnaley, Matthew, 'Queens Birthday Honours: Captain Gordon Vette J.P.', *New Zealand Herald*, 4 June 2007

Winder, Virginia, 'Lord Worsley Runs Into Troubled Times', Puke Ariki, www.pukeariki.com

Winder, Victoria, 'The Plunder of Parihaka', Puke Ariki, www.pukeariki.com

Woodd Richard and Hulbert, Jayne, 'George the Jack Russell dies saving kids', *Taranaki Daily News*, 2 May 2007

Young, Audrey, 'Naval visits unlikely till we accept', *New Zealand Herald*, 14 April 2010

Articles with no author credits

'Adulteration', *Daily Southern Cross*, 30 October 1871

'The August offensive–the Gallipoli campaign', www.nzhistory.net.nz/war/the-gallipoli-campaign/the-august-offensive, (Ministry for Culture and Heritage), updated 6 March 2008

'Battle accounts, Lieutenant Averill–New Zealand and Le Quesnoy', www.nzhistory.net.nz/war/le-quesnoy/battle-accounts-lt-averill, (Ministry for Culture and Heritage), updated 26 April 2007

'Doc. Averill', *NZ Truth*, Issue 1155, 19 January 1928

'Douglas Jolly', www.nzhistory.net.nz/people/douglas-jolly, (Ministry for Culture and Heritage), updated 1 April 2010

Editorial, *Auckland Star*, 28 November 1874

Editorial, *Daily Southern Cross*, 12 June 1871

Editorial, *Daily Southern Cross*, 2 September 1871

Editorial, *The Evening Post*, 25 July 1873

Editorial, *The Taranaki Herald*, 21 November 1874

'Erebus Tragedy: Myths and Reality,' *Dominion Post*, 12 February 2008

'Extra edition: They must not go', *Evening Post*, 16 October 1915

'Firefighter Tells I went from Hero to Zero', *New Idea*, 2007

'Geoffrey Cox', www.nzhistory.net.nz/people/geoffrey-cox, (Ministry for Culture and Heritage), updated 21 November 2009

'George to receive "Medal for Bravery" from SPCA', *New Zealand Herald*, 8 May 2007

'Inquest on the body of the mate', *Nelson Examiner and New Zealand Chronicle*, 8 September 1863

'It wasn't instructor's fault', *New Zealand Herald*, 18 April 2008

'Lecture by Polly Plum', *Daily Southern Cross*, 27 June 1871

'Lecture on female education', *Daily Southern Cross*, 1 August 1871

'The liberation of Le Quesnoy', www.nzhistory.net.nz/war/le-quesnoy/the-liberation-of-le-quesnoy, (Ministry for Culture and Heritage), updated 29 October 2008

'Local Intelligence. Wreck of the Brigantine Delaware', *Nelson Examiner and New Zealand Chronicle*, 5 September 1863

'Madame Yvonne', *Grey River Argus*, 15 October 1919

'Mrs Colclough's lecture at Otahuhu', *Daily Southern Cross*, 4 September 1871

'Mrs Colclough's lectures', *Wellington Independent*, 18 October 1871

'New Zealanders of the Year', *New Zealand Herald*, 6 December 2008

'Narrative of Events at the Bay of Islands', *New Zealander*, 19 November 1845

'A nurse's narrative', *Poverty Bay Herald*, 22 July 1915

'Obituary: Lady Grace Todd', *New Zealand Herald*, 5 January 2002

'Our lady's letter', *NZ Truth*, 15 November 1919

'Outrages alleged', *Grey River Argus*, 25 October 1919

'Parliament', *Grey River Argus*, 11 December 1918

'Polly Plum and Old Practical', *Daily Southern Cross*, 23 January 1871

'The Position of Woman', *Daily Southern Cross*, 10 July 1871

'Presentation of testimonials to the Maoris of Wakapuaka', *Nelson Examiner and New Zealand Chronicle*, 17 November 1863

'Purple Heart for brave George', *Sydney Morning Herald*, 8 May 2007

'Recalling good amid the grief', *Christchurch Press*, 22 April 2008

'Settlement in Northern Australia', *Otago Witness*, 29 July 1871

'Taranaki terrier to get UK's highest honour', www.stuff.co.nz, 21 January 2009

'Te Whiti-o-Rongomai', www.nzhistory.net.nz/people/erueti-te-whiti-o-rongomai-iii, (Ministry for Culture and Heritage), updated 9 November 2008

'Trampers' saviour honoured by city', *New Zealand Herald*, 13 October 2000

'Two deaths that made life precious', *New Zealand Herald*, 6 December 2008

Untitled article, *Poverty Bay Herald*, 20 January 1917

'The venereal vortex', *NZ Truth*, 26 February 1921

'A widow in gaol for debt', *Daily Southern Cross*, 18 January 1871

'Women in Print', *Evening Post*, 5 August 1915

'Woman Suffrage', *Hawke's Bay Herald*, 18 March 1893

'Wreck of the Brigantine Delaware', *Nelson Examiner and New Zealand Chronicle*, 8 September 1863

'Wreck of the Delaware', *Nelson Examiner and New Zealand Chronicle*, 12 September 1863

'WWII heroine ignored in honours list, says National,' *New Zealand Herald/NZPA*, 5 June 2007

Websites

www.army.mil.nz

www.battleofbritain1940.net

www.tepapa.govt.nz

www.conservation.co.nz

www.dpmc.govt.nz

www.erebus.co.nz

www.hollows.org

www.kakaporecovery.org.nz

www.nzetc.org

www.nzherald.co.nz

www.nzdf.mil.nz

www.nzhistory.net.nz

www.anzac.govt.nz/gallipoliguide

www.pdsa.org.uk

www.publicaddress.net

www.pukeariki.com

www.ruapehudc.govt.nz

www.stuff.co.nz

www.teara.govt.nz

Other

'Flight 901:Erebus 20 years On', *Sixty Minutes*, Television New Zealand Ltd, 1999.

'Goodbye to George', *Close Up*, Television New Zealand Ltd, 3 May 2007

Hansard, New Zealand Parliamentary Debates, Ministerial Statement–Erebus Inquiry, 25 August 1999

New Zealand Court of Inquiry Into the Circumstances Attending the Casualty Involving the Ship *Wahine*, T.E.V. *Wahine*, Government Printer, Wellington, 1968

Speech by Helen Clark, 8 August, 2005, Unveiling of the Plaque Commemorating Lt-Col William Malone, Grand Hall, Parliament–www.beehive.govt.nz

The Report of a Royal Commission to inquire into the Crash on Mount Erebus, Antartica, of a DC 10 Aircraft operated by Air New Zealand Ltd, Wellington, 1981

The Report of the Cervical Cancer Inquiry 1988, Government Printer, Auckland, 1988

The Waitangi Tribunal, *The Taranaki Report: Kaupapa Tuatahi*, 1996

Written findings of the inquest into the deaths of Antony McClean, Natasha Aimee Bray, Portia Caitlin McPhail, Huan (Tom) Hsu, Anthony Walter Mulder, Floyd Mariano Fernandes, Tara Rochelle Gregory. Heard in the Coroner's Court at Auckland, 15–19 February 2010.

Images

Section one:

Huria Matenga, courtesy of the O'Laughlen Collection, Alexander Turnbull Library, Wellington

Frank Worsley, courtesy of the J Thomson Collection, Alexander Turnbull Library, Wellington

Tangiwai disaster aftermath, courtesy of the Reeds Collection, Alexander Turnbull Library, Wellington

The *Wahine*, courtesy of the *Evening Post* Collection, Alexander Turnbull Library, Wellington

Hone Heke painted by Arthur McCormick, courtesy of the Alexander Turnbull Library, Wellington

William George Malone, courtesy of the James McAllister Collection, Alexander Turnbull Library, Wellington

Sir Keith Park, courtesy of the *Evening Post* Collection, Alexander Turnbull Library, Wellington

Howard Kippenberger and Charles Upham, courtesy of the War History Collection, Alexander Turnbull Library, Wellington

Nancy Wake, courtesy of the Australian War Memorial

Willie Apiata, courtesy of the *New Zealand Herald*, photographer: Alan Gibson

Section two:

Ettie Rout, courtesy of the JH Henderson Papers, Alexander Turnbull Library, Wellington

David Low and Gerry Harcourt Wybert, courtesy of the New Zealand Free Lance Collection, Alexander Turnbull Library

Sir Edmund Hillary and Tenzing Norgay, courtesy of the *Dominion Post* Collection, Alexander Turnbull Library, Wellington

Marilyn Waring and Sir Keith Holyoake, courtesy of the *Evening Post* Collection, Alexander Turnbull Library, Wellington

David Lange, courtesy of the *Dominion Post* Collection, Alexander Turnbull Library, Wellington

Te Whiti, courtesy of the Alexander Turnbull Library, Wellington

Kate Sheppard, courtesy of the Alexander Turnbull Library, Wellington

Dame Whina Cooper and Duncan McIntyre, courtesy of the *Dominion Post* Collection, Alexander Turnbull Library, Wellington

Sir Garfield Todd, courtesy of the *Evening Post* Collection, Alexander Turnbull Library, Wellington